Sketch Map of
EXMOOR MEETS,
PATHS AND TRACKS

Meets ....
Main Roads ....
Bridle &
Cart Tracks
Foot-Paths......
Boggy ground ....

GW00319423

EXMOOR
TRAVELLERS

The steep ascent from Lynmouth is almost complete. A coach and four on the Countisbury road

EXMOOR
TRAVELLERS

ROSEMARY ANNE LAUDER

ALAN SUTTON

Published in the United Kingdom in 1993 by
Alan Sutton Publishing Limited
Phoenix Mill • Far Thrupp • Stroud • Gloucestershire

Published in the United States of America in 1993 by
Alan Sutton Publishing Inc • 83 Washington Street • Dover • NH 03820

British Library Cataloguing in Publication Data

Lauder, Rosemary Anne
Exmoor Travellers
I. Title
942.385

ISBN 0–7509–0315–5

Library of Congress Cataloging in Publication Data Applied for

Endpapers: Sketch map of Exmoor from C. Aldin, Exmoor: The Riding Playground of England (*The North Devon Athenaeum, Barnstaple*)

Typeset in 11/15pt Bembo.
Typesetting and origination by
Alan Sutton Publishing Limited.
Printed and bound in Great Britain by
The Bath Press, Bath, Avon.

Contents

SCARLET PIMPERNEL MOTOR COACH AT MALMSMEAD

Illustrations

Illustrations

Acknowledgements

I wish to acknowledge the help that has been so generously given and without which a book such as *Exmoor Travellers* could not be written. A particular thank you to the staff of the North Devon Record Office and the Athenaeum in Barnstaple, and to David Bromwich of the Taunton Local History Library, each of which has been an invaluable source of material, and to the private individuals who have allowed me access to family papers and photograph albums.

ONE

The Early Visitors

In the year 918 those turbulent visitors to England, the Danes, having under the command of Earls Ohtor and Rhoald, entered the Severn and spread ruin and devastation along the opposite coasts of Wales, directed their course to Somersetshire and landed privately in the night by Porlock for the sake of plunder, but the inhabitants being timely alarmed gave them so warm a reception that the greater part were cut to pieces, and those few who escaped alive, were obliged to retire with greater precipitation to their ships.

HISTORY AND ANTIQUITIES OF THE COUNTY OF SOMERSET, REVD JOHN COLLINSON (1791)

These earliest recorded visitors to the shores of Exmoor received a warm welcome, much warmer than they would have liked or indeed expected. But they appear to be the only visitors that the inhabitants of Porlock 'saw off', and ever since those far off days Exmoor has been welcoming a motley throng. In these pages a handful are introduced, for Exmoor is a broad stage, and the players that have crossed its wide uplands are many and varied, coming with widely differing purposes, or no purpose at all, and leaving us with an assortment of impressions and recollections. Here is just the tip of the iceberg:

The said Chase is mountainous and cold ground, much beclouded with thick fogges and mists and is used for depasturing of cattle, horses and sheep and is a very sound sheep pasture. But a very great part thereof is overgrown with heath and yielding but a poor kind of turf of little value there.

Thus was Exmoor described in the Parliamentary Survey of 1651, and it seems that other visitors shared this uncharitable view: 'A solitarie place it is, the more commodious for Staggs, who keepe possession of it,' was the view of

Thomas Gerard of Trent in his PARTICULAR DESCRIPTION OF THE COUNTY OF SOMERSETT, written in 1633. True, it is the centre, the core of the ancient Forest of Exmoor that is being described, but there was little to appeal to visitors in those far off times – little, indeed, to appeal to the local population who obviously preferred to live around the edges of the moor, well away from the often severe weather conditions. Here is another view of life in the Middle Ages on Exmoor:

We shall probably not be rash if we think of wide stretches of moorland, treeless and desolate, bordered by dense forest, spreading over the low lands down to the sea, with here and there a cultivated clearing around the rude hall of a local lord, and the still ruder hovels of his serfs and villeins. The small population had to be fed and clothed by its own land, and warmed by the fuel provided by its own woods. Roads were almost unknown, indeed they were little needed. Occasional and unwilling expeditions had to be made to the shire-moot and the hundred court in the face of difficulties of travel. Beyond this it must have been rare for anyone but the lord and his personal following to have need to travel out of the place of his birth, and for the master the Severn sea was the more convenient access to the more populated country to the eastward. The life of man was spent in the struggle with nature to win sustenance from an ill-tilled soil, to gather during the summer months the food for the day and the store for the dark and unproductive winter.

HISTORY OF PARTS OF WEST SOMERSET, C. CHADWYCK HEALEY (1901)

Because of its barren and inhospitable nature, and lack of inhabitants, early travellers to the moor were few and far between. The earliest recorded visitor

EXFORD

was John Leland who travelled widely throughout the whole country between 1534 and 1543, but he provides only the barest details of his journey:

The residew of the way to Exford was partely on a moore and sumwhat baren of corne, and partely hylly, having many brookes gathering to the hither ripe of Ex ryver.

There is a litle tymbre bridge at Exforde over Ex brooke, ther being a smaul water.

Ex risith yn Exmore at a place caullid Excrosse a 3 miles of by north weste, and so goith toward Tyvertun a xij miles lower, and thens to Excestre a x. miles.

From Exford to Simonsbath bridge a 4 miles, al by forest, baren, and morisch ground, wher ys store and breading of yong catelle, but litle or no corne or habitation.

There rennith at this place caullid Simonsbath a ryver betwixt to great morisch hilles in a depe botom, and ther is a bridge of woodde over this water.

The water in somer most communely rennith flat apon stones easy to be passed over, but when raynes cum and stormes of wyntre it ragith and ys depe.

Always this streame ys a great deale bygger water then Ex is at Exford, yet it resortith into Ex ryver.

The boundes of Somerseteshire go beyond this streame one way by north west a 2 miles or more to a place caullid the Spanne, and the Tourres, for ther be hillokkes of yerth cast up of auncient tyme for markes and limites betwixt Somersetshir and Devonshire; and here about in the limes and boundes of Exmore forest.

From Simonsbath bridge I rode up an high morisch hylle, and so passing by 2 myles in lyke ground, the soyle began to be sumwhat fruteful, and the hilles to be ful of enclosures, ontylle I cam a 3 miles farther to a poore village caullid Brayforde, wher rennith a broke by likelihod resorting to Simonsbath water and Ex.

JOHN LELAND'S ITINERARY, JOHN LELAND (1543)

William Marshall, writing in 1796, is far more informative, and his comments seem primarily concerned with the state of the roads and the travellers he met en route. If the roads were as bad as he describes, it is perhaps not surprising that he managed to travel from Barnstaple to Swimbridge without meeting another wheeled vehicle! Marshall was travelling with a particular purpose – to report on the rural economy of the west of England for the Government. His conclusions, apart from the roads, appear to be more than favourable, and the Devonshire half of Exmoor at least receives some high praise:

The day is set in for rain; yet the appearance of the country is delightful beyond description. Perhaps rain, as varnish, mellows the views.

The roads in a shameful state: evidently injured by the hedges. Why is not the law enforced? In this country, where woodlands abound, and where coals may be had at a reasonable rate, no serious evil could arise were all the hedges in it shorn to their mounds.

Get a broad view of the rich and beautiful valley of Swimbridge. A fine back view of the Estuary and its banks: broad, but grand, and picturable.

Meet a pair of wheels: the first from Bideford.

A sweet country, but most difficult to be seen! Black limestone road, tolerably good.

Filleigh, Lord Fortescue's noble place, breaks at once upon the eye: a finely wooded basin. The timber abundant, and seemingly well set out. A herd of young cattle, and a flock of sheep, in the grounds about the house. The farmery large; bespeaking a suitable portion of demesne in hand. . . .

Pass a string of two-horse carts, guided with reins, in the Cleveland manner! Has a colony of Clevelanders formerly settled in North Devonshire, and brought with them their carts and horses?

Vile roads again: and in the neighbourhood of a great man's residence! But, perhaps, his lordship's lime work is the principal cause of the evil. The colour of the materials, and the state in which they at present lie, give them every appearance of roads to coal pits.

Mount a rich well turned swell, and enter the town of South Molton.

The town, which consists of a spacious well built market place, surrounded with inferior streets, caps a rotund hillock, situated among other hillocks of a similar nature, and wearing similar appearances; rich and beautiful in a superior degree.

Some wood in the valleys, but not one acre of unproductive land to be seen in the neighbourhood. One of the finest farming districts in the Kingdom. . . .

Bend to the left, from the Tiverton road; and enter narrow woody lanes, barely pervious to a carriage.

Break out of this pass, into other commons; and nearly approach the heaths of Exmoor, a narrow valley only intervening.

Exmoor, in this point of view, is without feature; appears as a flat, or at most, a tamely billowy heath. Its hills scarcely rise above the cultivated swells that environ them. This side of it, at least, has not a trait of the mountain character.

Enter and skirt a wide fern-grown common; large plots of fern now in swath. Also dwarf furze, and some heath. The soil deep and culturable.

The valley widens, and breaks into well soiled hillocks. The two parishes of East and West Anstey appear to be in a good state of culture.

Meet strings of lime horses, from Brampton lime works.

Lose sight of the Exmoor hills, but still keep the brink of the valley, having enjoyed a tolerably level road for seven or eight miles!

Leave the high ground, and descend into the valley. Stirring wheat fallows, with four oxen; the first oxen, and the first plough, I have seen at work in North Devonshire! Instance of watering grassland: the first I have observed in North Devonshire.

RURAL ECONOMY OF THE WEST OF ENGLAND, WILLIAM MARSHALL (1796)

Another early visitor who commented on Castle Hill was William Gilpin, travelling in 1798. He was not impressed by his lordship's improvements:

In our way we turned aside to see Lord Fortescue's place at Castlehill, where we didn't think we were sufficiently repaid for going so far out of our way. Lord Fortescue has improved a large tract of ground but without any great taste or connivance. Into one error he has particularly fallen, that of overbuilding his improvements. From one stand we counted 8 to 9 buildings. It is a much easier matter to erect a temple or palladian bridge than to improve a piece of ground with simplicity and beauty and give it an air of nature. One of the first buildings, the old castle upon a hill from which his place I suppose takes its name, stands beautifully. Little more I should think in the way of building would have been necessary. This lofty castle might be the object sufficient from almost every part of his improvements.

OBSERVATIONS ON THE WESTERN PARTS OF ENGLAND, WM GILPIN (1798)

Wild scenery seems not to have impressed these early visitors who, to a man, felt ill at ease among rocks and boulders, steep valleys and rugged heights. Even the views, when they comment on them, do not compensate for the arduousness of the roads. A more domestic landscape was more to their liking, and it was not until the era of Wordsworth and Southey that tastes began to change and 'scenery' became fashionable. Perhaps we have become accustomed

CASTLE HILL, THE SEAT OF EARL FORTESCUE

to the steepness of the hills and coombes, but the early travellers appeared to find them almost insurmountable. The Valley of Rocks was viewed as something supernatural, and altogether too awful and fantastic to be entirely natural – a view held up until the early years of this century:

The ruggedness and undulations of the roads in North Devon hitherto had not intimidated us, and we had retained our feats on our horses in tolerable security. Now it began to appear prudent to trust to none but our own legs. In descending into the glens with which the country is here furrowed to a frightful depth, a traveller would be distrustful even of a Welsh poney.—Between Combe-Martin and Linton the mountains exhibit an outline of much sublimity, and assume positions extremely picturesque. . . .

Still proceeding along chasm-like hollows, we at length began to ascend, and came to some elevated ground, whence we perceived rocky precipices at a distance, towards the sea, thickly clothed with wood. We had no idea that our road would soon turn suddenly to the left, and conduct us through this beautiful covert. From the summit to the bottom the mountains were overspread with oak, the branches below almost bathing in the briny current of the Severn. Their brows were at too great a distance above us to be seen through the foliage; in looking downwards to the shore, our apparent height above the main was increased by the occasional projection of the rocks, so that imagination had its full scope in the contemplation of this uncommon scenery. Every step was quite on romantic ground. New features, new embellishments, new combinations continually rose into view.—Our rapture rendered us insensible to fatigue, though we had long been obliged to follow on foot a devious, indistinct tract that now sunk with terrific steepness, now ascended with an almost insurmountable perpendicularity. If the reader would form some idea of its *ruggedness*, let him figure to himself the pavement of a street torn up by a plough, and the largest fragments of stone that are used retaining an erect position.—At length, wood and foliage vanished entirely, and a scene surprisingly grotesque and wild unfolded it,—a valley, bounded by large naked rocks, or rather fragments of rocks, piled one upon another. The heights on each side were of a mountainous magnitude, but composed, to all appearance, of loose unequal masses, which form here and there rude natural columns, and are fantastically arranged along the summits so as to resemble extensive ruins impending over the pass. Vast fragments overspread the valley, and, which way soever we turned our eyes, awful vestiges of convulsion and desolation presented themselves, inspiring the most sublime ideas.—An old man, mounted on a mule, who passed us and observed our silent wonder, announced to us that we were in the VALLEY OF STONES

OBSERVATIONS OF THE WESTERN COUNTIES, WM G. MATON (1794)

The clergy were also great travellers, and none more so than John Wesley, who was indefatigable – well almost – as this extract from his diary of 1744 shows:

Wednesday 18th

Between 5 and 6 in the evening we reached Minehead (from Sticklepath and Crediton) to find a general expectation of it among the people; about 7 I preached near the seashore to almost all the inhabitants of the place. Many of the gentlemen of the town were there and behaved with seriousness and decency. Thursday, 19th; Having a sloop ready which came on purpose, we ran over the Channel in about 4 hours. Some of our friends were waiting for us on the shore.

He ends his entry for that day: 'Oh for ease and a resting place! Not yet. But eternity is at hand!'

Wesley visited North Molton twice, on the first occasion in October, 1775:

In the evening I reached North Molton but being wet and tired and the people not having notice, I didn't preach until the next morning. A few I find stand steadfast here, though a neighbouring gentleman has threatened them and unless they will leave this way has turned them out of their work or farms, and headed the mob in person.

However, he found things improved two years later:

Between 12 and 1 I reached North Molton and finding the congregation ready, began immediately. There have been great tumults here since I was there before, but God has rebuked the storm. When the gentry would neither head nor pay the mob anymore, the poor rabble were quiet as lambs.

JOHN WESLEY'S DIARY (1777)

The Revd Richard Warner had no such missionary zeal and his WALKS THROUGH WALES AND THE WESTERN COUNTIES seem to have been undertaken purely for pleasure. He, too, found much to complain of in the state of the roads:

It should seem that the North Devonians were not very anxious after the company of strangers, for they certainly take the best possible means of preventing them from visiting this part of England, by the execrable state in which they keep their turnpike roads. Instead of making use of the advantages afforded them by their soil, and breaking the stone into small nodules which, pressed together by the weight of horses and carriages, would form adamantine and impenetrable roads, they carelessly sprinkle these public ways with masses of stone larger than a man's head, and leave them to time and chance to be broken and scattered, to the great danger of the horseman, and the discomfort of him who is in the carriage. . . .

To unravel the intricacies of the West-Somerset and North Devon cross-roads requires more sagacity, as well as patient research, than fall to the lot of most men; the traveller, therefore, who is not gifted with a large share of these qualities, will probably, in attempting to thread their maze at least double the actual distance between his stages. This, at least, has been my case; and notwithstanding the particular directions which the good people of this country, civil even to servility, afforded me, I have formed such a zig-zag line of march for these three days past, as, if measured, would certainly extend to sixty miles instead of forty, the real distance.

I will not deny, however, that I have been amply repaid for all these deviations from the right road, since many scenes of grandeur and beauty have discovered themselves to me in consequence, which I should otherwise have lost. . . .

Early in the morning of the 7th I left Minehead, intending to reach Linton, a village about twenty-five miles from that town, on the same evening. A deep shady road led me through Selworthy, and several other small hamlets, sequestered and picturesque in the highest degree. The inhabitants of these places, quiet in their manners, and ready in their offers of service, seemed to be formed for the peaceful retreats which they occupied. Far removed from the seats of *refinement*, as it is called, which is too frequently only an *elegant modification of vice*, the hinds pass their time, at least in honest simplicity; and having no artificial wants to supply, exhibit such an appearance of *contentment*, as gives them, in the eye of sober reason, a manifest advantage, when placed in comparison with the more refined classes of society.

WALKS THROUGH WALES AND THE WESTERN COUNTIES, REVD R. WARNER (1799)

It was said that the roads of Exmoor had hardly changed for a thousand years and that, until the coming of the turnpike roads in the second half of the nineteenth century, wheeled vehicles were a rarity and carriages virtually unknown except on the periphery roads. It was the pack-horse that kept goods on the move and it was the pack-horse that formed the old traditional routes across the moor – those deep, sunken, twisting lanes that can still be traced – from the mines at Molland to the little harbour at Combe Martin; from Dulverton to Minehead; and from North Molton to Barnstaple, a route in regular use until it was replaced by the turnpike in 1825, now in its turn replaced by the modern link road.

Meeting a train of pack-horses could be a frightening experience, as this extract from F.J. Snell's BOOK OF EXMOOR shows. The author is quoting from the Revd Wm Thornton's REMINISCENCES AND REFLECTIONS OF AN OLD WEST COUNTRY CLERGYMAN (1899):

'The road from Bampton to Dulverton had not been very delicate, yet nothing to complain of much—no deeper, indeed, than the hocks of a horse, except in the rotten places!'

LYNTON: VALLEY OF ROCKS

LYNTON AND LYNMOUTH FROM THE SUMMER HOUSE ON LYN CLIFF

The reader may be tempted to think this account improbable and exaggerated, but that is only because he has had no experience of similar conditions. The state of the West Country roads in the early part of the last century (by which time, it may be supposed, there had been attempts at improvement) has been well described by Mr. Thornton, and his remarks point to very primitive arrangements:–

'The roads were in a very bad condition. The old Roman roads, long neglected, were nearly gone. The Devonshire devious ways existed, which had been formed by the feet of pack-horses, who wandered right and left to avoid soft places until a track was made, against which banks were gradually thrown up to keep the cattle from straying from the adjacent fields (thus stereotyping for ever the wanderings of the horses).

These trackways were deeply water-worn and often shelved to a point in the centre, where large, loose stones lay roughly scattered. In my time, by day and by night I have traversed scores of such by-ways. In 1808 Mr. Vancouver, who was employed to make a report by the then Board of Agriculture, writes from experience of the horrors of a charge of pack-horses in one of these defiles. On they came without bridles or conductors, with their burdens brushing both sides of the deep-cut lane. There was nothing to be done except to turn and fly to a wider place until the string had passed on, led by some veteran charger who knew perfectly well where he was going.

The roads twisted considerably, as I have said, by reason of the wanderings of the horses, but as moors and waste lands were gradually taken in and enclosed, they twisted more and more, because the old trackway would often, in such cases, be disregarded by those who were enclosing, and the traffic would consequently have to go round the angles of a newly made fence until the old road could be resumed. There was practically no such thing on any but a very few of the main roads as a public conveyance. Everything was done on foot or on horseback. Even the very farmyard manure, and lime, and the earth from the bottom of the steep fields, were carried on horses' backs.'

Manure was, in fact, sent out in wooden vessels called 'dorsels,' and corn brought home on long crooks. In some places the ground was so steep that carriages simply could not be used.

The most superficial research into the habits of Old Exmoor will reveal the fact that the pack-horse was ubiquitous and indispensable. In 1765, when four of the Winsford bells were recast by Bilbie, they were broken up on the spot and the metal carried to Cullompton on pack-horses. . . .

Mr. Kingdon, of Simonsbath, told us that his aunt, when a young woman, drove a team of pack-horses from Southmolton to Corner Brake on Exmoor for the purpose of fetching slate. He can point out the old tracks, which do not correspond in the least with the modern roads, and are remarkable for their directness.

BOOK OF EXMOOR, F.J. SNELL (1903)

John Fortescue, a younger son of Earl Fortescue of Castle Hill, gives a good description of the vanished breed of pack-horse, which was much sought after. A good carrier could easily take around 250 lb, and sometimes up to 400 lb in weight, and strings could consist of twelve horses and more, though this was illegal. The leader carried a warning bell on his crook, or yoke, but as the driver was at the rear of the train, other road users had to look smart to get out of the way:

It can be little more than a century since Devon was, so to speak, opened up by rail and, almost simultaneously by road. In Devon, perhaps more than in most other counties, men travelled even at the beginning of the nineteenth century, in the saddle rather than on wheels. The roads, so called, were the old pack-horse tracks, the creation of 'crocks' rather than of men. What the 'crock' or pack-horse demanded above all was firm ground under his feet, and he made his deviations to assure himself of it. Compared with solidity under hoof, gradients were a matter of indifference to him. Only when he approached the water at the bottom of some deep combe or valley, and his load began to weigh heavily on his withers, did he seek a little relief. Then, the gradient being invariably very steep, he sidled down in a zigzag fashion, preferring the bare rock, if possible, for his foothold, and made the ascent in like manner after crossing the stream. There must have been trouble sometimes when the water was in flood after heavy rain, and hence came into being those quaint little narrow bridges with a refuge over the piers for hapless pedestrians. For it was no joke in the old days to meet a train of pack-horses. They occupied the whole of the road, leaving no room for a mounted man to pass, and they plodded on steadily, nose to tail, without a thought of stopping before any living obstruction. There were only two courses for a rider who encountered them—he must either jump the road-fence (not by any means always an easy thing, and very frequently impossible) or he must turn round and wait for the train to pass at the nearest gate or crossroad. But this difficulty passed away with the passing of the 'crock' himself. We hardly know what manner of beast he was. When I was a boy I remember a mare of my father's which was said by very old men to 'throw back' certainly to the old pack-horse. I can see her now, a long, low, not very comely creature of about fifteen hands, dark muddy chestnut in colour, with a crupper mark and horizontal dark stripes on her forelegs. She had a queer temper, but a strong constitution, and was a willing slave in harness. What survives of the 'crock's' work are the double corkscrew turns of the old roads on either side of the water at the foot of every valley; and even to-day these remain a terror to motor-cars. Only last year on the well-known hill of Langridge Ford I came across a car, containing a Glasgow tradesman and his family, hopelessly stranded in the double corkskrew. Every workman in the vicinity had rushed to the spot to offer help and, above all, advice (does not every true child of Devon prefer any job to his own and 'telling' to any job whatsoever?), but after an hour of talk and endeavour the hapless man was still no further on his way to Glasgow.

These roads, or at any rate the more dangerous portions of them, have in many cases been superseded by 'by-passes' or new constructions. Every facility is offered to visitors to hurry through our midst. Even on the newer roads, wherever the crossing of the head of a combe necessitates a sharpish turn, the old bank-fence has been taken down and replaced by wire. No doubt this makes for safety by enabling drivers to see if any other vehicle is approaching; but this work must have eaten up hundreds of thousands of pounds of the rate-payers' money, and the desired object of safety might be as effectively attained by the simple expedient of driving slowly round these bends. In a mountainous country, such as the *département* of the Alpes Maritimes in France, where abrupt corners are infinitely more numerous and more dangerous than in Devon, drivers are careful to maintain a moderate speed, though Frenchmen are at least as fond of hurrying as Englishmen. Is it necessary to encourage thus at great expense the prevailing lust after racing on the roads? As a matter of fact, the real way to see Devon is from the saddle, where you sit high enough to look over the fences. But one cannot put back the clock fifty years; and I must confess that since the advent of motor-cars I have seen more of the beloved county than ever before.

FOREWORD TO *DEVON COAST, MOORS AND RIVERS*, W.H. THOMPSON (1932)

Where roads did exist, they were not always considered an improvement. The steep hills, especially on the coastal routes, struck terror into the hearts of all who encountered them, and the hazardous conditions proved a deterrent right up until recent times when the modern engine and gearbox finally conquered the gradients. The skill of the driver, however, was not always equal to the severity of the incline, or to the sharpness of the bends:

The road from Countisbury to Lynmouth is not of a nature calculated to soothe the nervous. In a mile and a half it drops eight hundred feet, the last part being so steep that I have had to pass my arm round the rail of the box seat of a waggonette to keep myself from slipping on to the backs of the horses. It is true that the cushions were of that abomination known as 'American leather'; still, it needs a pretty good angle to disturb the balance of a sitting man even when American leather covers the matter sat upon.

Cut midway between the sea and the rocky ridge of the Torrs that separate the Channel from the glen of the Lyn, this road commands a

LYNMOUTH: GLEN LYN

LYNMOUTH: COUNTISBURY HILL

view that is excelled by few highways in the kingdom. The hillside sinks so abruptly to the sea that you cannot see the beach below— you look right down upon the waters of the bay patched with shifting light and shadow. At your back the huge mass of the Foreland, stained brown and pink and red, seems to shut out all the eastern world; westward the view is bounded by the heights of Lynton. Lynton itself never looks more picturesque than from this 'cornice' road—at sunset the effect is quite aerial. Then the rather too obtrusive hotels (not to speak of Mr. Newnes' new mansion on the hill top) are marvellously softened by the subdued light; hard angles vanish and staring windows become absorbed in the misty blue. The Valley of Rocks Hotel with its wings and turrets becomes the palace of a magician, and Lynton might be a city of the Thousand and One Nights.

On the seaward side of this road nothing but a low bank of turf and stones prevents coach and passengers rolling down the giddy height on to the beach. In places, indeed, this bank hardly seems high or substantial enough to be an efficient protection, and one wonders what would happen if the horses bolted and ran the heavy vehicle against it. I remember once asking the driver if there ever had been an accident. He replied in the negative, but casually added that a *wheel* had come off a few days before. Evidently as it was the off wheel the matter made no impression upon him. 'Suppose it had been the near wheel?' I suggested. He smiled and looked thoughtful.

The incident reminds me of a remark made by an artist friend, a man of some eminence in the old Water Colour Society. I once tried to persuade him to take a coach ride from Minehead to Ilfracombe, and strove to calm his fears by saying that accidents were almost unknown. 'Accidents!' he exclaimed, with a humorous twinkle in his eye; 'they never call anything an accident in North Devon *unless somebody is killed!*'

EXMOOR, J.L.W. PAGE (1890)

TWO

Unusual Visitors

*A*h the joys of the open road! The delights of travelling before everyone *travelled. The adventures of these early visitors – the sense of wonder at new scenery, of never knowing what was around the next corner – makes marvellous reading when tinged with nostalgia for that vanished Exmoor, that land of rough tracks and poor cottages where folk stayed put from one year's end to the next, and knew everything that was going on around them and nothing of what was happening farther afield.*

Today's visitors can drive all around the moor and see most of it in a day – they see everything, yet in reality see nothing. It was these early travellers with their slow and leisurely pace who really explored and learnt about the Moor. By far the best way of exploring and learning about Exmoor is on foot, on horseback, in a carriage, or even behind a travelling puppet show!

Visitors of any kind were something of a rarity to Exmoor and foreigners (proper foreigners that is) almost unheard of. One wonders what the local farmers made of Mr Elihu Burritt, an American, who in 1834 decided to walk from London to John o' Groats, and then from London to Land's End, and back!

His diary entry of 15 July 1834 reads:

This was an anniversary to me of special interest. This day, a year ago, I set out on my Walk from London to John O'Groat's. During the year I have measured the distance on foot between that extreme and Land's End, and from the latter to this point on my way back to London. In addition to this pedestrianism, I have written a book of four hundred pages, travelled several thousand miles by railway, lectured about sixty times, and performed other labors with foot, tongue and pen. So, on the whole, it has been one of the busiest as well as most enjoyable years of my life.

ON THE ROAD

Starting from Dulverton, and deviating to Molland, he compares the Exmoor scenery to the prairies of his homeland. He seems to have been favourably impressed, though the locals may not have cared for the description 'aborigines', and the inhabitants of Timberscombe would have been surprised to find themselves moved to Devonshire. With true American thinking he finds it hard to understand why the gentry of Exmoor are so lacking in ambition, preferring to remain on the family estates rather than carve a name for themselves in the outside world. England of the feudal ages is how Exmoor appeared to this transatlantic visitor. But how must he have appeared to Exmoor?

13

Wednesday, July 13th. . . .

Passed along the eastern edge of Exmoor, ascending and descending hills all the day long. I am persuaded that the impression generally prevails among Americans who have never visited this country, that *moors* are an English edition of our prairies, bound in heather, gorse and ferns, instead of our prairie-grass; that they present the same surface, sometimes a dead level, and occasionally rolling into a gentle ground-swell like the sea, when no wave on it arises high enough to don a white crest. This idea is a mistaken notion. Although there are moors in England as level as some of our Western prairies, there are more, if the figure will hold, like a sea of mountains. Exmoor, for example, is piled cloud-high with dark, sullen hills, some of which are called beacons. Whether any warning fires were ever kindled on their grim and ragged summits, or whether they took the name from serving as guide-posts over the waste, the local history does not decide. One of these beacons is 1668 feet above the sea; a second, 1610, and a third, 1540. The valleys correspond with these bleak and lofty elevations in wildness, which the lonely streams make more impressive with their dash, splash and gurgle in their crooked channels among the rocks. This moor has been the pasture and roaming-ground of a peculiar set of aborigines, which have retained their primitive characteristics in face of modern improvements. The old red forest-deer still run as wild in some parts as if they had the range of the Adirondack Mountains. The 'Exmoor pony,' too, represents a breed of horses that the Druids lassoed before Julius Caesar was born, and the 'Exmoor sheep' doubtless are natives of equal antiquity.

The scenery on approaching Timberscombe was the most delightful of the kind I ever saw. For full three miles I descended a winding glen by a regular Devonshire lane; and realised more vividly than ever before the meaning of the term. It was very narrow, occasionally not wide enough for two donkey-carts to pass each other. In some places the lane was cut into the rock to the depth of several feet. This solid wall was supplemented by another of earth and stones in alternate layers. The top was planted with all kinds of bushes and shrubbery, which had not been trimmed for years. Out of this high and motley bank towered a thick growth of trees of great height. The bushes grew inward until they completely arched the pathway, and the trees formed another arch or vault far above. Here and there an opening in this green roofage would let in a patch of light, that gave a remarkable vividness to the sides of the hedge and set all kinds of fantastic shadows playing upon the ground before you. Once in a while you caught a glimpse of a heather-crowned hill through the branches of the trees; but frequently for many rods the side scenery would be entirely shut out. Then you came to a portal in the wall and looked through it, as through a window in a long-vaulted gallery, when a scene of indescribable loveliness met your eyes. Through one of these green, wicker-work casements you saw fields as soft and green as lawns lying up against the lofty hills, all framed with hedges, like so many nests of new-born verdure; from another, a basin deep and beautiful, holding in the sun, within its daisy-flecked rim, a bright stream rounded into a pool and beyond, where the leaping brook, laughing at the shallow dam, ran between level banks, mottled cows lay ruminating with quiet eyes, looking complacently at their faces in the water. Take it all in all, this was the longest natural gallery I ever walked through, with more dioramic views or vista-posterns opened in each side.

At about dusk, I came out upon the sea at Dunster, an old-fashioned town crowned with a castle, and sleeping under the watch and ward of several tall and stalwart hills standing around it, like gigantic sentinels in bear-skin caps. It is an interesting place altogether. The superincumbent strata of modern civilisation are rather few and thin here. England of the feudal ages crops out in their characteristic aspects. The castle is as large and strong as life. It not only crowns but seems to rule the town. The main street appears to belong to it like its shadow. The houses are drawn up in a row on each side, like a well-disciplined band of retainers, to present arms and touch their hats when the great baron passes. This castle was erected in Elizabeth's day, and ran the gauntlet of the stirring events that filled the succeeding century. It stood a siege and a severe bruising in the Civil War. It entertained Charles II., in its best guest and banquet room, and William Prynne with coarser roomage and fare, — a

HIGH STREET, DUNSTER

thoughts and deeds and memories its sieve retains to the credit and remembrance of names that were promised immortality and expected it from the local homage and influence they commanded! How much higher than a castle set upon a hill, how much more lasting than a mausoleum of marble with engraven arms of Norman device, is the memory of two lines, or two words, or two acts the world has learned by heart, and repeats as guide-thoughts for human life!

After tea, faced directly eastward again, and walked on by the sea to Blue Anchor, a quiet, cosy, little watering-place with a large and comfortable inn, and a few lodging-houses for visitors who prize rest and retirement while drinking at the blue fountains of sea air. Both the land and water views from this point are truly delightful and interesting from their remarkable contrasts.

A WALK FROM LONDON TO LAND'S END AND BACK, ELIHU BURRITT (1834)

A happy view of Exmoor comes from the pen of James John Hissey who spent several weeks of each year driving himself and his wife around the countryside in his phaeton. In 1886 they visited Exmoor and had little but praise, although they found it quite easy to get lost and commented on the lack of signposts, and of roads that led everywhere and ended up nowhere. He describes a way of travelling and exploring the moor now lost to us.

Pleasure steamers travelling down the Channel from Bristol and across from Wales were still very much part of the scene, but Mr Hissey was not in favour of sharing Exmoor's beauty spots with these noisy day trippers, which he seems to indicate should be kept for his sole enjoyment! He must have had good weather for most of his stay, for he is one of the few writers to comment on the sunsets, often such a marvellous spectacle from the coast and hills of Exmoor:

member of the Long Parliament, whom Cromwell shut up here for penitential meditation and political improvement of mind. It now belongs to the *Luttrell* family, which has absorbed several genealogical rivulets of ancient nobility into itself, and represents and enjoys their dignities and estates. An American, even well-read in English history, will come upon many an establishment of this territorial extent and social position with a kind of surprise tinctured with sadness. This has been my own experience frequently. How is it that a name of such all-absorbing local influence has made so little history outside the circumference of a family estate, or a memory of so short a radius! One feels somewhat at a loss to decide at the first, unexpected sight of such a baronial castle, whether it comes from his own ignorance of noted celebrities, or from the owner's want of personal merit, that he has to inquire, 'Who lives in that mansion in the park yonder?' He asks this self-deprecatingly as if he ought to know; and, ten to one, he is answered as if he ought to know; and the villager thus questioned looks at him with an expression half wonder and half pity, as if he said, or would like to say, 'I thought everybody knew the Squire.' In Time's great sifting of the generations, how few

From Ilfracombe to Lynton is one of the most delightful drives imaginable. The country you pass through has the quality of being exceedingly varied; in the twenty miles or so you have almost all classes of scenery, though the wild and grand predominate. It is in truth a glorious road; along secluded dales and over steep hills our way led us, affording grand prospects of rocky cliffs and picturesque bays, with peeps of the glistening sea beyond, then across far-spreading moorlands till we came to a small hamlet in a deep hollow, and there we found a very tiny inn, as befitted so diminutive a place. But, tiny though it was, the little wayside hostel had stables attached, so we decided we would rest our horses there. As for ourselves we expected nothing, the place looked so humble; but one must not always judge by outside appearances. I went inside to try the ale, for the weather was hot, and if it was to be had tolerably good a draught of ale would be very acceptable. To my surprise I was asked into a 'wee' sitting-room, very 'wee' truly, but neat and clean, and with a window in proportion to its size: this looked out upon a pretty gurgling stream, the quiet plashing of its waters being the only sound that broke the stillness. The room was refreshingly cool, and we were glad to rest in it out of the glaring sunshine. The ale proved excellent, and so we ventured to inquire what else in the way of refreshments we could have, the result being that we had a repast of ham and eggs. When all else fails, the inevitable everlasting ham and eggs can generally be procured even at the humblest house of entertainment.

On again, over bleak uplands, wind-swept by the salt-laden ocean breezes, we continued; the light bracing atmosphere was most exhilarating, a life-giving air, soft yet strong—there is no tonic in the world like a walk or drive upon some moorland height, and if near to the sea so much the better. The horses gloried in it as much as we did; they kept sniffing the thin buoyant air, tossing their heads, and prancing as though they had only just come fresh from out of their own stables, and had not already done some five hundred miles of hard work. . . .

And next we came to far-famed and justly renowned Lynton, one of the most beautiful spots on the British coast, I think I may safely say *the* most beautiful. Indeed, it would be hard to imagine anything more perfect or to conceive beforehand such a wonderful entrancing combination of wood and hill, of rock and river, of bold crags and land-bound sea, for this latter is terminated on the horizon by the blue changeful line of the Welsh coast. We found here an excellent hotel, as was to be expected so far from railways, situated on a wood-crowned height, with fir-clad slopes stretching down to a golden ocean, which latter repeated the glories of the luminous sky above. It was impossible for us to remain indoors that evening, so we wandered out amongst the tossing pines and rare shrubs that led from the garden of our inn downward towards the sea. What a gorgeous prospect lay before us as—

The evening sun descending
Set the clouds on fire with redness,
Burned the broad sky like a prairie,
Left upon the level water
One long track and trail of splendour.

No words—least of all any words of mine—can describe the tranquil loveliness of these Devonshire sunsets, the commingled glory of sea and air, of earth and sky. A peace as of paradise seems to rest on all around. The palpitating atmosphere is charged with a flowing light permeating everywhere, diffusing its golden glory all around. Living so much in cities as many of us do, we little observe the wonderful sky scenery that this cloud-loving England of ours everywhere so plentifully affords; possibly we have grown to forget that such a thing exists. Beautiful, even spectacular sunsets are by no means of rare occurrence. Indeed, so accustomed to these had we become during our out-door life that we looked forward almost each day to the evening, as a matter of course, for scenic sunset effects. . . .

Next morning we drove through the wild Valley of the Rocks; grand and wild it certainly is, but the impressiveness of its desolation was spoilt the day we were there by numberless excursionists laughing and calling to each other: these had evidently been landed by a steamer—steamboats are as great sinners as railways in this respect; at any available beauty-spot they mercilessly disgorge crowded hordes of trippers, the most provoking part being, as I have said before, that these said excursionists would enjoy themselves equally well in less choice localities, they only want an outing and fresh air, somewhere where they can run and romp about, shout and make themselves happy and thoroughly tired. Impressive scenery requires to be beheld in all its solitary grandeur; there is one thing it will not stand, and that is noisy cheap-trippers; they strike a chord totally out of harmony with it; their proper place is on Brighton beach, or upon Margate or Ramsgate sands, where at any rate they are in accordance with their surroundings.

Leaving, then, the Valley of the Rocks to the tender mercies of the careless and care-for-nothing crowd, we proceeded onwards over rough and hilly roads in search of tripperless lands, and we found them. We explored a tract of country that abounded in glorious prospects, wide open and free: these by-ways are not in the guide books, and so we were, as my wife said, 'severely left alone,' and for the rest of the day so lonely was our road that we met not a soul. . . .

We had a good deal of rough driving, exploring an utterly unknown land (to us), and a most romantic one it proved to be. After much pleasant wandering we determined at last that we would strike inland, and endeavour to find, if possible, a route over the moors back to Lynton. A rather hazardous venture this, as the country was bleak, the roads were hilly, narrow, and guiltless of sign-posts, and the inhabitants were few. The latter of course, by some strange ordinance of fate, are never visible when wanted, and in their absence we could only guess by the direction the roads took—often, by the way, changing confusedly—whither they might lead us. But such uncertainties, provided the weather be fine and the horses fresh, are very enjoyable, and though no adventures may occur, there is still always the feeling that one of some kind is just possible. . . .

Eventually, after losing ourselves more than once, and after many aimless wanderings, we got safely back to Lynton, not however till the gloaming had overtaken us. These country by-paths (in Devonshire above all other places) seem to lead everywhere and yet nowhere in particular: often they start fair and with golden promises—therein the danger lies—but trust them not farther than you can see; it is just as likely as not that after leading you along hopefully for a mile or more they will without any apparent reason gradually grow worse and worse—so gradually that you keep on trusting that at each bend things will improve—till they land you helplessly upon an open moor, the road vanishing into a mere track, which in its turn again loses itself in half a dozen minor paths utterly impracticable for carriages; or it may be after numberless windings, just when you feel sure you are arriving somewhere, you will arrive at an old disused quarry, much to your disgust, or perchance you may find your road suddenly ending at an out-of-the-world farmhouse (not an uncommon occurrence), in all of which cases there is nothing for it but to retrace your course—a not very inspiriting proceeding. Such at least is our experience of country by-roads, more especially in hilly districts, where moorlands and quarries abound; but for all this they are delightful wandering; they lead one into the very heart of the land, into remote unheeded unknown spots, whose primitive simplicity carries the wayfarer back long centuries. It is another England they take you to, an old-world land where superstitions, quaint customs, and long-forgotten prejudices linger still, and kindly hearts abound.

ON THE BOX SEAT, JAMES JOHN HISSEY (1886)

Another delightful book, full of interesting anecdotes and reminiscences, is A.G. Bradley's EXMOOR MEMORIES. Written in 1926, it begins with his first impressions when, as a schoolboy, he was packed off to the house of a Revd gentleman who lived at the village of 'Windycombe', there to undergo some extra tuition. It appears to have been more of a holiday than anything else, with lessons including hunting and fishing:

It was pitch dark when the Barnstaple train started on its then slow, halting, two hours' journey along winding valleys and across and beside purling streams, all of which would have aroused my interest had they been visible. It was also raining, though it had been freezing in Wiltshire, and when I reached Barnstaple it was pouring cats and dogs. Alighting on the cramped little uncovered platform, with its dim oil lamps, I peered anxiously into the gloom through the glistening raindrops for some friendly sign. I knew, of course, that I was to be met for the twelve miles' drive up into No-Man's land. But no welcoming form appeared, and I wandered forlornly up and down, every scrap of the adventurer's spirit dead within me. I

LYNTON AND BARNSTAPLE RAILWAY

went out through the booking-office and saw several carriage lamps flashing in the rain outside, but none of them apparently flashed for me.

A year or two later I should have got a porter to shout out if there was a carriage for Windycombe. I was hardly up to that yet, and in truth was slightly dumbfounded, as in despair I stood in the doorway wondering what was to become of me. Suddenly a short, stout, rather elderly, white-faced individual in a clergyman's tie and a top-hat emerged out of the gloom and to my inexpressible relief enquired if I was I. Relief, however, was mingled for a few seconds with amazement. Could this podgy little grey-haired man have played in the eleven at Marlborough and rowed in the Oxford eight a dozen years ago, or indeed at any time? The problem, however, was quickly solved.

'There is a fly for us here,' he said, 'and the driver told me to look out for you.' A fat boy, a little older, apparently than myself, came up at this moment. 'This is my son,' said my rescuer. 'He is going to Windycombe and will be your companion there; he is a Marlborough boy.'

I did not recognise him, but there was nothing odd about that in a big school, and when I also claimed that honour it was, of course, greeted all round as a happy coincidence.

So thankfully, my trunk collected, I got into the two-horse fly with my rescuers and we rolled off into the night. After perhaps half an hour of steady trotting we relapsed into a walk and maintained that sober pace for at least as long, dragging apparently up an interminable ascent. It was a warm night for the season, and the window was down on my side. The rain had ceased and the moon was rising into a stormy sky, while dark wooded hills rose high on either side. But the air was full of unaccustomed sounds, of which the loudest note was a stream tumbling below over a rocky bed, with the gleam of its foam showing in the hollow beside the road. White spouts of water seemed to be constantly leaping into the road with plash and gurgle. Even in the shifting moonlight it appeared to me altogether another world from any I had ever known, and a thousand miles away from the Wiltshire downs and water-meadows I had left that very morning.

After a time we crawled up the street of a long village where for the first time I inhaled the pungent smell of peat smoke, strange, of course, to me. Then we broke into a trot for a mile or so along a bare level plateau, and with all eyes agog I could see ahead of us, beneath the now clear and full moon, a waving barrier of high hills. I felt instinctively this must be Exmoor, and with the same sort of exaltation that, at a more sophisticated period of life, one gets from one's first glimpse of the Rocky Mountains or the Alps. I turned to my protector, but he didn't answer. He was, in fact, sound asleep and faintly snoring. It didn't matter much. I knew him well in later years at his plain, late-Georgian mansion on the clays of Essex, a hospitable, kindly, commonplace, East Anglian squire. His white tie and tall hat were merely relics of the times when he was a young country parson before he inherited his broad acres. He was East Anglian to his finger-tips, of a type probably now passed away, that liked a level country, had no use for hills nor any yearnings for mountains. At any rate I am quite certain he had not the faintest interest in Exmoor looming under either sun or moon.

Indeed, it was well he was asleep, for we now began scrambling up or pitching down a succession of stony steeps that were in actual fact not surpassed in Devonshire, and what more could be said? Horses, fly and driver seemed all wrought up to a very agony of extreme endeavour. At length after plunging down a final precipice through a dark wood, we rolled across a narrow stone bridge, under which a mountain stream was thundering in spate, a new sight and a new sensation altogether to me. But the Essex squarson slept through it all, luckily for him. He used to tell me in after years how when he went back to Barnstaple next day in the rector's trap he shuddered at the perils he had safely surmounted in his dreams; while the rector's man, William, who had never seen anybody get out up or down a hill in his life (they never did in that country), said he had to use physical force to prevent this eccentric and nervous 'up-countryman' from hopping in and out a dozen times.

A mile of comparatively smooth road, with the river roaring just below us, and the high hills, beneath the moon looming larger and larger, brought us to a standstill before a drive gate. The stout squarson woke up with a—'What's the matter?'

'I think we are there, sir,' said I. 'And the man's got down to open the gate.'

'Tom, do you hear? We are at Windycombe. Why, I believe the boy's asleep!' (With an air of bland surprise.)

The fat boy had, in truth, been asleep ever since he had consumed a bag of buns soon after leaving Barnstaple. He and his father were, in truth, of a thoroughly sound but pachydermatous breed. I more than once enjoyed their kindly hospitality in succeeding years, and I always recall T— Hall as the very quintessence of mid-Victorian materialistic, matter-of-fact comfort. There wasn't a nerve or an idea in all that happy household. On those undulating, wheat-growing, clay lands, the fat boy's family lived and moved and had their being, and filled their place immaculately. They are all dead and gone, every one of them, or I should not say this much here.

A hundred yards down a woody drive and we pulled up short in a blaze of dazzling light that streamed from the open door of the Rectory. Intimately as I came afterwards to know that long, picturesque, perpendicular, laborious road, I have never forgotten those early boyish impressions of my first adventuring it in the moonlight of a stormy winter night. I could feel and even smell as well as see it. It was another world to any I had known. In Wales or Scotland I should have expected surprises and been proportionately excited. But here, in practically the very next county to Wiltshire—for Windycombe touched and overlapped the Somerset line—it seemed a wonderful thing, and still more so next morning when daylight lit up the beautiful and to me novel scene.

Exmoor Memories, A.G. Bradley (1926)

These early visitors certainly found some novel and interesting ways in which to travel around Exmoor. For a few weeks in the summer of 1927 Walter Wilkinson became a wandering Punch and Judy man, earning his keep as he went from village to village. He seems to have found this much to his liking: the joys of the open road, and the freedom and 'away from it all' feeling. In the introduction to his book, THE PEEP SHOW (1927), Mr Wilkinson describes how it all came about:

In this way I hoped to live a healthy outdoor life and a life full of changing interest. I hoped to detach myself from the gruesome commercialism, this ridiculous race for fortunes, this vulgar materialism which is filling the world with 'things' instead of ideas, surrounding us with greasy engines and raucous noises instead of Divine Thoughts and Songs of Praise. Root-ti-ti-toot! This was altogether an excellent idea of Mr Punch's and I accepted his intriguing profession with enthusiasm and joy!

Their first performance was given at Minehead with apparent success, but the two adventurers found themselves threatened by the attitude of the other (professional) buskers and decided to leave the town behind:

After our varied day of travelling by train, by two steamers, and tramping by road, and after the excitement, not to mention the hard work of performing in Minehead, we were very pleased with our quiet camp on the hillside overlooking the valley and the rising downs beyond. We pottered about our jobs until the moon rose, and the bright stars appeared silently in the clear sky, then we crawled into our tent on all fours and lit our lanterns. We sat side by side in our respective sleeping-sacks, with our heads touching the roof of the tent, our backs against the end, and our feet at the door. There was no room left for even a puppet. We completely filled the tent. We were snug.

'Ho! Ho!' said William, 'this is all right, my boys! Have a piece of chocolate!'

'Ha! Ha!' said I, 'I like this. I would rather be here than in one of those lodging-house rooms, among the iron railings and pavements of Minehead.'

'Rather,' agreed William, 'this is better than a stuffy interior. I can't stand those furnished rooms which look like a nightmare on the hire system.'

'Yes,' said I, 'and here we are free of all those screaming advertisements of teas, those hysterical announcements of beastly char-à-bancs trips, and those altogether ever so much too much important advertisements of motor spirit.'

'Why,' said William, 'we live in a poem. Out here on the moonlit hillside among the foxgloves and bracken, we enjoy the experience of living like romantic mountebanks in a picture.'

Here he pulled out his ancient flageolet and began piping sweet Elizabethan airs, whilst I searched in the box for the interesting works of William Shakespeare in one volume. To read them? Oh dear no! I wanted to mend a large hole in one of my socks, and I remembered that when packing I had seen the darning wool just under the volume.

Presently we settled down to sleep, while outside in the moonlight a wandering nightjar serenaded us. Inside the tent we breathed the fresh air fragrant with thyme and lady's bedstraw, on clumps of which we had made our beds. It was not long before William began to snore, a thing which I never do myself.

And on to Porlock:

As we wandered along among the rolling hills we made our plans for the day, and accomplished the first of them by arriving in Porlock before the carpenter had closed his workshop for the week-end. Here we bought some long wooden battens and screws, as we had decided to screw up the framework of the theatre permanently and travel with it ready for use, so that we could strike up a performance in as little time as possible.

The carpenter expressed his admiration for Punch and Judy shows, and hoped that we would perform in the town. In return, I expressed my admiration for his carpentry and said that I rather envied him.

'I would rather have your job,' he said, 'to get about from one place to another instead of being stuck in this workshop for ten hours a day, year in, year out. Yes, you do a show in Porlock this evening. The band will be out about half-past eight, and if I were you I should get in a show or two before then, about seven. I shall come along and have a look.'

We decided to adopt his advice, and after some wandering and waiting we got a pitch for the tent in a meadow between the town and the sea. Here we spent the afternoon in carpentry and eating until it was time to get into the town with the show.

We had been advised to interview the policeman; he had been recommended to us as 'a good sort,' so we were not so nervous as we might have been, especially when we found him at his cottage in his shirt-sleeves. We mentioned to him the discreet place well away from the traffic of the narrow High Street where we had thought of pitching the theatre, but like the carpenter he began to arrange the affair for us.

'Now if you goes higher oop the street,' he said, 'you'll get more people like. They'll all be out there this evening, and if you was to goo oop outside the Castle Hotel—now look 'ee 'ere, sir, if I wur you I should speak to the landlord there, he's a good sort, and I lay he'd let you set oop outside on his piece there. That's it, you goo oop along and arsk 'e.'

There was a kindliness about this suggestion which we could not resist, and we soon pulled up to the Castle Hotel and asked for the permission. The landlord entered into the affair with spirit. 'What, do a Punch and Judy show, boy! Yes, certainly, anywhere you like, and good luck and a good living to you.' He sent out a boy to show us, to a hair's-breadth, the very best stand we could take, and there accordingly we set up the theatre.

It was not long before curious eyes were upon us, and passers-by halted in their promenade. We caught several housewives with their prams and babies out for the Saturday shopping. Sober workmen leaned up against the opposite fence smoking their pipes; several groups of promenading flappers took their stand before us arm-in-arm, and consequently the young bloods were pulled up too.

PORLOCK

Children clamoured round us wanting to know how much it was to pay, and the simple generous-minded ones rushed off to get pennies, while the horrid clever ones stayed to see it for nothing. One boy offered us a penny on the spot, but William took his pipe from his mouth, refused the coin, and uttered that honest slogan—'Work first, pay afterwards.'

With the first notes of the squeaky music someone in the audience began to laugh; at the first appearance of John Barleycorn the children gave a wild shout, and when Martha, his wife, looked out of her window and then fell out, the whole audience was captured and guffawed in unison. Through a hole in the curtains I could see a smiling crowd entirely blocking up the High Street, and as the performance proceeded I could hear the pleasant sound of pennies clinking into the bag as William went the rounds. . . .

I then changed places with William, and after waiting a little for a change of audience, his puppets began their performance and I took my turn at the collecting. But first of all I became one of the audience; I tried to imagine myself a native of Porlock and that I had just seen The Peep Show for the first time. That is one of the tragedies of a puppet-showman, after all his hard work he can never see his own performance.

As soon as the puppets appeared, the chattering crowd became quiet and attentive, closing in round the theatre, and this is what we saw.

The old country man and the modern artist begin the scene with a discussion on music. The yokel sings an ancient folk-song which the artist despises as an old thing, a very old song. For his part he has modern tastes; he only sings the very latest thing, and accordingly, in humorous caricature, he sings, 'Come into the Garden, Maud,' which does not impress the old yokel in the least. The song finished, the yokel thinks he would like his portrait painted, whereupon the artist produces his easel and canvas, and with a real brush and real ink, actually draws a good portrait of the old man, who, not realising how clever it is for a puppet to draw at all, says it is not a portrait, that, in fact it is nothing at all but a lot of black lines. Naturally this

leads to an argument, and then to a fight, which is ended by the old man seizing the canvas and smashing it over the artist's head, so that he finishes up wearing it as a collar.

As I went round with the bag every face was wreathed in smiles at this scene, and I overheard constant remarks, such as, 'That's all right, ain't it!' 'Ain't that all right!' 'I never see one like this before,' while two men were so impressed by its unusual quality that they supposed we were only doing it 'for a bit of fun like.' It must have been William who gave rise to that idea; it was either his dignified way of collecting as he strolled round smoking his pipe, or it may have been his new boots which flashed like unblemished gold and had come from Piccadilly, an unusual shopping district for Punch and Judy men.

By this time the town band was assembling and trying its instruments, so we packed up our theatre and felt very much the 'real thing' as we retired into the bar of the Castle Hotel to cool our burning throats with a glass of Devon cider. Here we talked with a horsey individual who understood well the requirements of our show, and gave us useful information about the road to Lynmouth and the places at which we could show on the way.

We arrived back at our camp as it was growing dark, with the feeling that we had had quite enough adventures for one day. It is good fun doing puppet-shows, but after all it is something of an upheaval and a nervous strain for two respectable young men to become travelling showmen, and we were glad to crawl into our dog-kennel of a tent, slip into our sleeping-sacks, and enjoy a sober supper of buns and cocoa. There in the corner of the field we were in snug quarters, but criticised the farmer a good deal who had put us into this stony field instead of the one we had set our hearts on, a soft meadow full of new-mown hay.

As we took our supper we produced our collection bag and wondered how much there was in it. It was a good weight of coin, but would not amount to very much if it was all copper; we were not greedy, but still, we had our living to get. We tipped the bag upside down and searched the coins for silver, but alas! they were all brown ones! We counted them out, arranging them in piles of twelve on a saucepan lid, and found that we had seven shillings and twopence halfpenny. Not a large amount, but sufficient for our simple expenses for the day. One old lady when contributing had held up her penny to William and said, 'I've got a penny for you. I've been holding it so long in my hand that it's quite warm.'

It was as well Mr Wilkinson had a companion, for it took several hours of back-breaking toil to reach the top of Porlock Hill:

We went out of the town by the natural, steep hill, leaving the toll road of easier gradient to the ridiculous motor-cars. Porlock Hill is one of the longest and steepest in the country; a famous hill, and in ascending it with our show we felt that we were making history. Had a Punch and Judy show ever climbed this road to the high moors before?

About a hundred yards from the first sudden turn of the hill we pulled up to consider the situation. A passing motorist, smiling from among his easy cushions had called out to us, 'That looks like hard work,' and we soon found ourselves in profound agreement with him. We left The Old Encumbrance tilting in the gutter and walked away with an offended air. In the magnificent view and some cigarettes we sought forgetfulness; after the cigarettes we found it necessary to draw the view in our sketch-books, and after that our rest was prolonged while some huntsmen and a pack of hounds, who all smelt our vehicle, wandered by. Then, in sober mood, but with grim determination, we pulled off our coats, rolled up our sleeves, and were about to put ourselves to the task again when we heard a shout of alarm behind us and saw, on the steep corner of the road below, a motor-car come to a sudden stop.

We ran down the hill immediately to investigate the trouble and found that the car, jibbing at the steep gradient, had begun to run backwards, that the owner was clinging to the brakes, helpless, and that his frightened wife was clinging to him. Having mastered this particular piece of hill ourselves we set about the rescue of the car

PORLOCK HILL, GRADIENT 1 IN 4

with superior feelings. William and I, as proper vagrants, have philosophic objections to motor-cars, and we were amused at this ridiculous engine being beaten by the good Exmoor Hill. We blocked the wheels with stones, when the wife descended in a hurry of relief and the engines were set going again. But for all their roaring and blustering and imitation energy they were futile, and it was not until the two Punch and Judy men had applied their shoulders to the wheel that the thing was reversed and set safely on its way back to find the special motor road. As we stood on either side of the car talking to the driver, he suddenly, amid profuse thanks, flung out both his arms, seized our hands and left in each a shilling. We felt inclined to blush and refuse the tip; we protested, but the man was away, and after all, were we not men of the road with our livings to get? We put the shillings in our pockets and credited them to the account of our earnings for the day.

Refreshed by this incident, and with a renewed belief in our powers, we set off again determined to achieve what the car had failed to do. For two steady hours we took it in turns to pull or push, and although we tried a hundred different ways the problem was always the same, each step was a good stiff pull. Luckily it was our constant duty as poets to admire the view, and as artists we had to make a drawing or two; it was simply as hungry men that we took our lunch at noon instead of one o'clock. Our constant thought and conversation was of reducing the outfit, but if we discarded the theatre we should earn no pennies to live on, and if we turned out the camp we would lose our lodgings. The only rejection I could think of was the interesting works of William Shakespeare in one volume, but they were securely packed, and we struggled on with our complete load.

The country became wilder and higher. The hedges disappeared and we trudged an open road with moorland all around us, a moorland thick with heather, bilberry and bracken. At the road to Exford we halted, brought to a standstill by the immense beauty of our surroundings. We left the gritty road and wandered about the heather trying to approach the wild ponies and foals, but the pretty things tossed their long tails and manes and trotted away from us. We could hardly tear ourselves away from this view of sea, of rolling downs, and the vast stretch of moorland all sombre greens and browns in the grey day. But time was wearing on, and, as we hoped to reach a village where we could earn some pennies, we returned to our task. We drank in the high, keen air, as refreshing as spring water, and despite the hard pulling we progressed buoyantly. At three o'clock, after nearly four hours' pulling, we came to the summit and a sign post, finding ourselves only three miles from Porlock instead of the five which we had imagined. We had thus progressed at about three quarters of a mile an hour.

It was a relief to arrive at the road leading down to Oare and Brendon. It was a further joy to find a notice there stating that it was unsuitable for motor traffic, and that consequently we might expect it to have a natural surface, that it would be free of garages, spirit advertisements, and dumps of rusty old tar barrels. We were not disappointed; it is a perfect road that runs down to Oare and Brendon and the Doone country, such a road as might have existed for all time, and not a modern, narrow-minded affair, suitable only for machines. This was a free road, a thing of ups and downs, of turns and twists, of banks and hedges; a road good enough for tramps and pedlars, for poets, for philosophers, a road for us, William and me with our vagrant, gipsy theatre.

THE PEEP SHOW, WALTER WILKINSON (1927)

THREE

The Coming of the Tourists

The Revd W.H. Thornton, who described himself as an 'old West Country clergyman' was a great traveller around and over Exmoor, and he has left us his 'Reminiscences and Reflections' which are not only delightful but also instructive, if somewhat rambling! His carefree youth seemed to consist of sport and visiting, first as a pupil and later as a curate, and he was appointed the first rector of Simonsbath in 1856. Here he gives vent to his feelings on the new breed of visitor beginning to invade the countryside:

In those days everybody was hospitable. No one ever begrudged you anything. You could eat, drink, sleep, shoot, fish, ride, or walk almost anywhere you pleased, and the pleasure afforded by your company was thought to be payment enough. The truth is that the country was not at that time opened up, and people were glad of the companionship of anyone who was a little different to themselves.

The strange creatures who sometimes now emerge from our large towns and scatter themselves broadcast over the face of the poor country, have much to answer for. They are apt to corrupt our simplicity; they diminish hospitality; they curtail freedom. I have entertained grave suspicions that some of them are rather idiotic. They occasionally seem to be under the influence of a delusion. When they walk through our well-cultivated corn-fields they imagine themselves to be pioneers in a trackless wilderness. I have seen them holding on firmly to the pavement of our country towns by aid of alpenstocks. They have come to my house along good turnpike roads provided with compasses. They will stare into the entrance of a rectory house, inhabited by a graduate of Oxford, under the delusion that it is the wigwam of a savage. They

will flatten their noses against our drawing-room windows the better to observe the manners and customs of the aborigines within. All this it is very easy to smile at. But when they enter a time-honoured temple of God, apparently to discover what strange superstition forms the worship of the place, and on learning that it is only Christianity after all that is believed in, clatter out in the middle of a prayer to chatter loudly outside, it is difficult to refrain from reproving them.

It is really hard to exaggerate the extent of this evil or to describe the mischievous consequences which it has produced.

Sir Frederick Knight helped me many years ago to break up a party of these people who had entered the lawn at Glenthorne, and were looking in at the study windows, gaping at a statue of Venus, which my old squire, Mr Halliday, had brought from Italy. They probably mistook it for an image of the tutelary deity of the house, if, indeed, they had heard of tutelary deities, which is doubtful.

These people are apt to leave gates open, so as to allow cattle to wander. They grub up our wild plants by the roots, light fires in dangerous situations, trample on crops, bestrew nature's loveliest scenes with scraps of most greasy paper, sing very vulgar songs very much out of tune, and make themselves generally disagreeable.

They have caused much of the old Devonshire hospitality to disappear. When they come in large numbers simplicity goes, and in our watering places virtue is apt to go with it.

REMINISCENCES AND REFLECTIONS OF AN OLD WEST COUNTRY CLERGYMAN,
REVD WM H. THORNTON (1899)

By the early years of this century, the picture had changed dramatically. The age of travel, and of leisure, was upon us. The age when people could afford *to take time off and explore their own country, when the motor-car revolutionized everything:*

Until comparatively recent times Exmoor was a practically unknown land, frequented chiefly by sportsmen, for hunting is the great sport of the West, and the district is the last habitat in this country of the wild red deer. But the advent of railways and the improvement everywhere of the roads have brought the district to the knowledge of hundreds of thousands of tourists and visitors, who are invariably charmed with its varied and lavish beauty, and many return year after year, bringing others in their wake.

Of the towns of the Exmoor Country, Dulverton and Lynton may be approached *via* the Great Western branch line from Taunton to Barnstaple, and Minehead and Dunster by a similar line from Taunton to Minehead; while Lynton, with its sister village of Lynmouth, is also served by coach from Minehead; and Dulverton may be reached from Minehead by road, the drive being a very fine one.

RED GUIDE, WARD LOCK (1911)

It is unrealistic to bemoan the fate that overtook the villages, in particular Lynmouth and Porlock. Lost and deserted villages are to be found in Cornwall, Wales and on the north coast of England, where a few ruined cottages are all that remain of a community that found it could no longer continue to live once its livelihood had gone. Trawling no longer supports a family, and the herring shoals that brought prosperity to the Channel fishermen deserted these coasts some time in the early nineteenth century. Without the coming of the visitors, Porlock, Lynton and Lynmouth would have dwindled away to almost nothing.

One writer who visited the twin villages in the early days of their transition from fishing villages to tourist mecca quite succumbed to their sylvan charms, although he seems not to have approved of the new cliff railway completed in 1890:

The steepest part of the road passes through a copse which entirely conceals Lynmouth until we are close upon it. A sharp bend at the very foot, and the Lyndale Hotel comes suddenly into view and the bridge that spans the clear flood of the river. On this bridge everyone must loiter, for from it the gorge is seen to great advantage, notwithstanding the presence in the foreground of sundry not very picturesque cottages. By the way, were I the owner of the Lyn banks, I would, methinks, allow no house to be put up that did not harmonise with the scenery. Hard, angular buildings, unbroken by gable or projection, seem hardly the thing in the loveliest glen in Devon. Something in the style of a Swiss *châlet*, now, would surely be more appropriate than these stern, straight walls and steely-looking roofs of slate. Look how the slopes descend, scarred with rock and scree, or half covered with oak and ash! Is it not like an Alpine pass? And, if you walk a little way up the valley, other vistas will open out, each lovelier than the last—wood, and coppice, and rock—until in the distance, far away against the sky line, the eye rests at last upon some breezy croft high up on the borderland of Exmoor.

Lynmouth consists of a single street, facing the river. Every other house is a hotel or lodging-house, but the general appearance of the place is not unpicturesque, and some regard has evidently been had for the romantic surroundings. At the bottom is the rough little harbour overlooked by a square tower, the tints of which have mellowed so rapidly under the hand of Time, that it might be three hundred years old at least. As a matter of fact, it dates but from the latter end of the last century. It was the gift of a General Rawdon, a resident to whom this village on the Lyn owes no small debt. It is a copy of a tower on the Rhine.

Lynmouth was once a thriving fishing village—not innocent, too, of smuggling. For some reason or other, that most fickle of fish, the herring, chose to make the bay its favourite resort. For ten years—from 1787 to 1797—they could almost be dipped out of the sea in baskets, and were even used as manure. Then the shoals suddenly departed, and, for a long time now, have never visited the bay in anything approaching the former quantity. So Lynmouth has to fish for other fry, and does it pretty successfully. Every year does the shoal of visitors increase, and, probably, they pay better than the herrings.

The twin towns—or villages—are connected by the steepest passenger railway in the kingdom—perhaps in the world. It runs straight up the hillside at a gradient of one in one and a quarter. The motive power is hydraulic, the water being contained in a tank beneath the cars, which are connected by wire hawsers. The descending car raises that ascending, and danger is reduced to a minimum by automatic brakes. This Cliff Railway, as it is called, was initiated by Mr. Newnes, the journalist, whose mansion we noticed just now upon the hill top above. That it—the railway, not the house—should add to the beauty of the surroundings is of course impossible, but it must be admitted that every care has been taken to make it as unobjectionable as may be. It is in a deep cutting, and, except when seen from the sea, is not much *en évidence*.

EXPLORATION OF THE COAST OF NORTH DEVON, J.L.W. PAGE (1893)

It must be said that the inhabitants managed to adapt very quickly and to catch on to what was to become not only their 'bread and butter', but for many their 'jam and cream' for the first time in their lives.

The poets (Southey, Coleridge, Wordsworth and Shelley) all came to Exmoor around the turn of the nineteenth century, and this account of the beginning of tourism by J. Presland gives us an interesting insight of what might have happened had they remained, instead of departing to immortalize the English Lakes:

and we are of the twentieth century, and have discovered the beauty of docks and harbours and tall factory chimneys and railway stations, under the guidance of Whistler and Brangwyn and such folk, and we do not fret at laying a railway through Perthshire or the Lake District, because railways are fast becoming almost as romantic and old-fashioned to us as stage-coaches (in these days of aeroplanes and automobiles); but at least let us remember that it is to the nineteenth century that we owe that acute appreciation, not only of the visible beauty of the world, but of the spirit that lies behind it, that personal and intimate character of places which is one of our dear possessions. Mountains and woods, cliff and cove, have become to us a truism of

THE CLIFF RAILWAY BETWEEN LYNTON AND LYNMOUTH

beauty, but let us at least be grateful to the generation which first dared to see more in the boundless Scotch hills and moors than 'savage and disgusting country,' or to compare the pinnacles of the Alps to human handiwork—greatly to their disadvantage. And the small absurdities, the 'ruins' that they loved, the 'abbeys' they erected, were only part of that general half-conscious striving to apprehend and express the spirit of romance with which we are still moved in our own day, which Kipling expresses in his own fashion and Conrad in his, down to the small-change of literature which struggles for expression in our magazines and periodicals.

So when Shelley and Coleridge and Wordsworth came to Lynton, and found it beautiful, and nearly decided to live there and be the poets of Devon instead of the poets of the Lake District, it was because they found in it that quality of beauty which they needed; and when, a little later, Lynton was 'discovered' by one or more people of wealth—notably by Mr. Coutts, the banker, who built houses there and hotels, and began to noise its beauty up and down the London world—it was just the outermost ripple of the vast disturbance of the French Revolution which touched the little spot, part of the free new eager spirit which sent men questing for a loveliness they could neither make nor control, and of which they must be humble and passive spectators, and part also of vast causes and changes, which drove Englishmen to seek their holidays within their own shores.

LYNTON AND LYNMOUTH, J. PRESLAND (1918)

Almost at the end of his travels along THE NORTH DEVON COAST, C.G. Harper is also favourably impressed with Lynmouth, although he is gently mocking of the writers who so exaggerated the scenery:

One misses something in approaching the place, nor does one ever find it there. It is something that can readily be spared, being indeed nothing less than the usual squalid fringe that seems so inevitable an introduction to towns and villages, no matter how large or small. There are no introductory gasworks in the approaches to Lynmouth; no dustbins, advertisement-hoardings, or flagrant, dirty domestic details that usually herald civilisation. The customary accumulated refuse is astonishingly absent: mysteriously etherialised and abolished; but how is it done? In what manner do the local authorities magic it away? Do they pronounce some incantation, and then, with a mystic pass or two, abolish it?

Lynmouth would have pleased Dr. Johnson, who held the opinion that the most beautiful landscape was capable of improvement by the addition of a good inn in the foreground. We have grown in these days beyond mere inns, which are places the more luxurious persons admire from the outside, for their picturesque qualities—and pass on. Dr. Johnson's ideal has been transcended here, and hotels, in the foreground, in the middle distance, above, below, and on the skyline, should serve to render it, from this standpoint, the most picturesque place in this country. One odd result of this complexion of affairs is that when a Lynmouth hotel proprietor issues booklets of tariffs, including photographic views of the place, he finds that all his choice pictures contain representations of other people's hotels. This is sorrow's crown of sorrow, the acme of agony, the *ne plus ultra* of disgust. Resting on the commanding terrace of the Tors Hotel, seated amidst its wooded grounds like some Highland shooting-box, I can see perhaps eight others; and down in the village a house that is not either a hotel, an inn, or a boarding-house, or that does not let apartments, is a shop. And I don't think there is a shop that does not sell picture-postcards! There are some few very fine villas, situated in their own grounds, on the hillsides, but whenever any one of these comes into the market, it also becomes a hotel.

About the time when Lynmouth and Lynton were . . . first rising into favour, the poet Southey came this way, and wrote a description that has ever since been most abundantly quoted. But it is impossible not to quote it again, even though the comparison with places in Portugal is uncalled for, absurd, and entirely beside the mark.

Thus, Southey: 'My walk to Ilfracombe led me through Lynmouth, the finest spot, except Cintra and Arrabida, which I have ever seen. Two rivers join at Lynmouth; each of these flows down a combe, rolling over huge stones, like a long waterfall. Immediately at their junction they enter the sea, and the rivers and the sea make but one uproar. Of these combes, the one is richly wooded, the other runs between two high, bare, stony hills, wooded at the base. From the Summerhouse Hill between the two is a prospect most magnificent—on either hand combes and the river; before, the beautiful little village, which, I am assured by one who is familiar with Switzerland, resembles a Swiss village.'

And so with a host of others, to whom the hills 'beetle,' the rocks 'frown savagely,' the sea 'roars like a devouring monster.' And all the while, you know, they don't do anything of the kind. Instead, the hills slant away beautifully up skyward, the rocks, draped with ivy and moss and studded with ferns, look benignant, and the sea and the Lyn together still the senses with their combined drowsy murmur, as you sit looking alternately down upon the harbour or up at the wooded heights from that finest of vantage points, the 'Tors' terrace, after dinner, when the lights in the village and those of the hillside villas twinkle in the twilight, like jewels. The poetry of the scene appeals to all, except perhaps Miss Marie Corelli, who, in the 'Mighty Atom,' does not appear to approve of it. This, of course, is very discouraging, but the inhabitants are endeavouring to bear up; apparently with a considerable measure of success.

Mr Harper had a mischievous sense of humour and a sense of the ridiculous, as he has proved in his writings, and ends his long description of Lynmouth and Lynton with this interesting thought:

There is always, in the summer, a cheerful stir in Lynton, and the railway has by no means abolished the four-horsed coach that plies between Ilfracombe and this point, and even on to Minehead. But when the close of the season has come and the holiday world has gone home, what then? The hotel-keepers and all the ministrants to the crowds of visitors must surely, to protect themselves from sheer ennui, institute a kind of desperate 'general post,' and go and stay with each other, on excessive terms, to keep their hands in, so to say.

THE NORTH DEVON COAST, C.G. HARPER (1908)

The early tourists were undoubtedly a hardy breed, if the following proposed itinerary is anything to go by. We join this expedition at Lynton Cottages, and thence to Watersmeet – all before lunch:

He will next visit the *grounds of Sir W. Herries*, which occupy the ravine through which the W. Lyn comes hurrying under *Lyn Cliff*, where it falls in a cascade; and if inclined to extend the ramble, a path will lead him up the stream nearly 1/2 m.; and 'perhaps nowhere,' says 'the Sketcher' (Blackwood), 'is to be found so much beauty of painter's detail, of water, foliage, stones, and banks, within so small a space.' The *Filmy fern* grows here abundantly, and the turf is chequered by the ivy-leaved *Campanula*, while the sweet-scented *Lastroea oreopteris* and *L. Filix mas paleacea* attain an unrivalled luxuriance ('FERNY COMBES,' 1856). Having fully explored this romantic retreat, he is advised to mount his pony and proceed up the gorge of the E. Lyn, or *Lyndale*, as far as the junction of 2 branches of the river, at a spot prettily named *Waters' Meet* (about 2 m., to which there is also a path along the rt. bank through the woods, but it is longer and more fatiguing). Here the scenery is most beautiful. The sides of the ravine are covered with woods, the haunt of the wild deer of Exmoor, and rocks in various places protrude as cliffs, or lie coated with moss under the oaks on the hillside. Far below, where the foamy torrents unite, stands a rural little cottage, the property of the Rev. W.S. Halliday of Glenthorne. From this spot you can proceed 1/2 m. further to *Ilford Bridges*, and thence cross the hills to *Lyn Cliff*, or, if on foot, you can climb from Waters' Meet at once in the same direction. The view of Lyndale from these heights, and the grandeur of the surrounding country, will be ample recompense for the fatigue of the ascent. After contemplating the depths of the valley, raise your eyes to the dark ridges of Exmoor stretching in deep purple E. and W. and N. to the sea. At the close of the autumn these desolate hills have donned their most gloomy garb and are in character with wintry skies. . . . Cross the W. Lyn and return to Lynton by a horse-road opposite Lynbridge. He will probably have returned to his hotel about the time for a luncheon. He can next proceed to the

WATERSMEET BRIDGE, LYNMOUTH

. . . *Valley of Rocks*. This wild and interesting scene is about 1 m. W. of Lynton, and approached either by the *North Walk* above the cliff, or by a carriage-road. The former should be selected. It is a path cut midway along a rapid slope of about 700 ft., and forms a narrow terrace commanding a fine sea view, the cloud-like mountains of Wales in the distance, the gorge of the E. Lyn (in perspective), and a sweep of dreary coast terminated by the *Lynmouth Foreland*.

After skirting the sea for about a mile you come to a gap in the hillside, and through this colossal portal, between 2 masses of bare pyramidal limestone, you enter the *Valley of Rocks*, which may well astonish the traveller when they first break upon his view, rising abruptly from the face of the slope in crags and pinnacles. In a few minutes he will be passing below them. Southey describes it as 'a spot which is one of the greatest wonders indeed in the West of England. Imagine a narrow vale between 2 ridges of hills somewhat steep: the southern hill turfed: the vale, which runs from east to west, covered with huge stones and fragments of stone among the fern that fills it; the northern ridge completely bare, excoriated of all turf and all soil, the very bones and skeleton of the earth; rock reclining upon rock, stone piled upon stone, a huge terrific mass. A palace of the pre-Adamite kings, a city of the Anakim must have appeared so shapeless, and yet so like the ruins of what had been shaped after the waters of the flood subsided. I ascended with some toil the highest point; 2 large stones inclining on each other formed a rude portal on the summit. Here I sat down. A little level platform, about 2 yds. long, lay before me, and then the eye immediately fell upon the sea, far, very far, below. I never felt the sublimity of solitude before.'

One of these rocks is known as the *Chimney Rock*, and another, which throws its shadow on you as you turn into the valley, by the whimsical name of *Rugged Jack*. Having threaded this pass, the traveller will find himself upon the greensward of the valley itself; the *Castle Rock* rising like some Norman ruin on the rt., and the crag called the *Devil's Cheesewring*, or *Cheese-press*, from the hillside opposite. He is now in the heart of the stony vale, which descends obliquely towards the sea, but at a great elevation, and will probably rest to contemplate the wild and singular scene. He may ponder meanwhile on the probability of a mighty torrent having once rolled through this trough-way to the sea, and of the land having been afterwards upraised to its present position. A human interest also attaches to this lonely glen. From time immemorial it has been known as the *Danes*; and tradition acquaints us that a party of those marauders, when pursued from a neighbouring village, were here overtaken and slaughtered; and in connection with the legend it is a curious circumstance that a number of bones have been discovered in cutting a path up the Castle Rock.

You will ascend the Castle Rock. This, at one time, was a feat requiring some agility; but a few years ago one John Norman received permission from the lord of the manor to make paths and destroy rocks that he might levy toll on the stranger. It must be allowed that he has executed his work in a masterly manner. The walk along the cliff is worthy of a Telford, and the path up the Castle enables the veriest coward to ascend to the summit; but the native wildness of this huge ruinous crag is gone for ever. On all sides it is covered with rubbish; a terrace has been levelled near the top, and, sad to relate, the weather-beaten rocks have been actually hewn into seats and tables. Here may be seen a block of several tons weight, so nicely balanced, that a heave of a crowbar would send it thundering to the sea; and at the base of the cliffs the mouths of several caverns which are said to extend a long way underground, and can be visited by one of Norman's paths. The view is, of course, very extensive, and in a westerly direction the eye ranges from *Duty Point* and *Lee Bay* to the great promontory of *High Vear*.

MURRAY'S HANDBOOK (1865)

The British Medical Association used to, and probably still does, travel around the countryside holding its annual conferences in a different area, on which it published a report, a kind of medical guide book. In 1907 it produced a BOOK OF THE SOUTH WEST, printed for its seventy-fifth annual meeting held in Exeter. Here is what they found to say about Exmoor in general, and Lynton and Lynmouth in particular:

CASTLE ROCK, LYNTON

Exmoor is warm and very equable wherever shelter can be obtained and there is abundance of it in the rather narrow valleys under its steep hills—with heavy rainfall but a quickly drying soil, a great deal of sunlight, bracing air, bare heights but beautifully wooded hollows in shelter. The soil is formed of Devonian grits, shales and sandstones. In 1906 Lynton recorded 2000 hours of sunshine—only beaten by Torquay with 2026. However, records of rainfall (kept at Arlington for 1881–80) were 52.9 inches—beaten only by Altarnun on Bodmin (58.11) and Princetown on Dartmoor (72.2).

The sanitary district of Lynton includes some of the loveliest scenery in England. It varies in altitude from the level to 800 feet above it, and it is generally sheltered from all winds except the north and north-east. The valleys are exceptionally sheltered from wind. Lynton stands 430 feet above the Bristol Channel, Lynmouth near the shore. The climate is warm and equable, Lynton being more bracing than Lynmouth. The soil consists of Devonian slate, grits and sandstone, and is very porous, whilst the steep hills and rapidly descending valleys provide excellent natural drainage.

The average annual rainfall from 1898 to 1906 has been 43.28 inches, and the rainy days 186; in 1906 there were 2,000 hours of sunshine, a very high record.

The district is a very healthy one: between 1891 and 1900 the average general death-rate was only 12.31 per 1,000, the average death-rate under one year 112.10 per 1,000 births, and the average zymotic death-rate so low as 0.58 per 1,000. Longevity is remarkable here, as it is at Ilfracombe; during the ten years, 1891–1900, 42 per cent of the deaths occurred over 60, and of these many were at 70, 80 and 90.

Phthisis is not common, and is seldom associated with haemoptysis. In the early stages cases do well here if resident in the higher part of the district. Scrofula and tuberculous diseases (excluding phthisis) are also not common. Bronchitis is fairly prevalent; cases seem to do best at the higher levels. Pneumonia is not common, and seemingly bad cases make good recoveries. Asthma is not common. Acute renal dropsy is very uncommon. Chronic albuminuria is not frequent.

Anaemia and debility are not common. Heart disease, valvular and otherwise, is prevalent. Acute rheumatism, which is usually mild in type, is also prevalent. The steep hills seem to be largely responsible for the production of cardiac dilation. Neither rheumatoid arthritis, neuralgia nor gout are common. Sleeplessness is unknown, except in some cardiac cases. Skin diseases, especially eczema, are fairly prevalent.

'The almost abnormal longevity of the inhabitants testifies to the suitability of the climate for residence of old people.' It is well adapted to those who have come home from tropical climates; in summer Lynton is delightfully cool and fairly bracing.

BOOK OF THE SOUTH WEST, BRITISH MEDICAL ASSOCIATION (1907)

But we can't leave those two magical villages on such a prosaic note. Better to end with this lyrical passage from Mr Presland, who certainly fell under the spell of the Lyn. He tells of his escape from the popular Watersmeet:

On the loneliest, loveliest day in early summer . . . I made haste to leave the river path and the sheltering trees and climb the road to Brendon, a road as steep and hot, as stony and glaring, as I have ever climbed. Up and up I went for half an hour, seeing nothing but the banks and hedges on either hand; every turn in the road I thought was the last span that would bring me out on the hill-tops, and every turn of the road showed me another. But at last I stood above Brendon, and before me spread the moors, brown and purple in the sunlight, and the little old grey church of Brendon just below me, in a slight dip of the high ground.

The woods of the Lyn Valley climbed to my feet, and I sat down in the shade of the outermost fringe of trees to eat my lunch, and dream and muse, and doze away the first hot hours of the afternoon. I sat looking down over the valley; below me and to right and left the green spikes of the larches were aflutter in the wind; before me rose a great bare shoulder of hill, outlined sharply against the blue. Overhead the sun was blazing, but in the wood the sunlight hung mistily among the trunks and branches of oak and birch; it looked as

THE FISHING LODGE AT WATERSMEET

lay on the dry, clean turf and moss, looking up at the cloudless sky; a solitary swallow hawking far up seemed no bigger than a fly, and a brilliant green fly on a leaf above me, buzzing turbulently, seemed portentously big and important. I lost my sense of space and time and of the world in relation to men, set, as it were, as the background to me, and I slipped into a world which belongs to the birds and the mice and the moles, and the fish in the clear stream below; I watched the chaffinches and thrushes, and a little grey ash-tree near me which was full of linnets, delicious, sleek, grey, sweet-piping, busy little birds, sliding and skimming in and out of the tree, a little home of song and love-making, of intimate and familiar life. I heard a cuckoo calling from the thick woods of the valley below, like the note of a bell, very far away. I noticed the unopened buds of the ash shining like silver against the flawless blue sky; it seemed to me I had lain there a hundred years looking at them, and hearing the thin song of the linnets, in a world entranced from movement or the passing of time. And then I fell asleep.

LYNTON AND LYNMOUTH, J. PRESLAND (1918)

if the wood were filled with tremulous sunlit water, rather than with air and sun. The air from off the moors was keen and very sweet. I

FOUR

Border Country

*L*eaving Mr Presland asleep on his moorland height, we must depart from the Lyn valley by the more regular road and climb the notorious hill to Countisbury and the Somerset border.

Mr Harper, again, with his gentle humour, takes us up the hill and pauses to ponder on the origins of the name of Countisbury:

The six miles or so of the North Devon coast between Lynmouth and Glenthorne, where it joins Somerset, may best be explored from Lynton by taking the coast-line on the way out, and returning by the uninteresting, but at any rate not difficult, main road. The outward scramble is quite sufficiently arduous. The road sets out at first, artlessly enough, full in view of the sea. It rises from about the sea-level at Lynmouth, steeply up to a height of some four hundred feet at Countisbury, passing beneath a rawly red, new villa built on the naked hillside by a wealthy person whose hobby it is said to be to visit a fresh place almost every summer, to build a house, and then to move away. The name of the house I forget; suffice it to say that the Lynmouth people, gazing with seared eyes upon it, know it as 'The Blot.' Below, on the left, is the strand known as 'Sillery Sands,' which sounds like champagne. Some style them 'Silvery' sands, others even 'celery'; but they are not 'silvery'; and no celery, and still less any champagne, is to be found there.

At the summit of this steep road are the few scattered cottages of Countisbury, or 'Cunsbear,' as the old writers have it. Few would suspect that the names of Countisbury and Canterbury have an origin nearly akin; yet it is so, 'Kaint-ys-burig' – the 'headland camp,' being closely allied to the original Kaintware-burig, the 'camp of the men of Kent.' But to the writers of a generation ago, who wrote in a blissful age when there were no students of the science of place-names to call them to account, the name was set down as a contraction of 'county's boundary.' Distinctly good as this may possibly be as an effort of the imagination, it is not borne out by facts; for the county boundary did not exist at the time when the name came into being, county divisions having been settled at a much later date. Moreover, the boundary is a good three miles distant. Old Risdon, writing in 1630, is even more delightful. He takes what the scientific world styles the 'line of least resistance,' and gaily dismisses it with 'probably the land of some Countess.'

But there is not much of this Countisbury, about whose name there has been so much said. Just a bleached-looking, weather-beaten church, the 'Blue Ball' inn, typical rural hostelry of these parts, and the school-house. For the life of me, I do not know which drone the loudest on a hot, drowsy summer afternoon; the bees or the school-children at their lessons—the bees, I believe. And that is all there is to Countisbury, you think. This, indeed, is the sum-total of the village.

THE NORTH DEVON COAST, C.G. HARPER (1908)

Very nearly at the border itself is the Old Barrow earthwork, to most of us a series of humps and mounds in the earth, but beauty is in the eye of the beholder, and to an enthusiast of such things it appears differently:

About four miles E. of Lynmouth, and just in Devonshire, overlooking the combe of Glenthorne, W. of County Gate and on the seaward side of the road, is *Old Barrow (Burrow) Camp*, 'one of the most perfect camps in Devonshire'. It has a triple vallum and fosse;

the inner area of about 90 feet diameter, which is square with rounded corners, is defended by two valla and two ditches: but outside this is a circular vallum, 9 feet high on the S. side, and 6 feet on the sea side, with a fosse after an interspace of 16 yards in width. The entrance to the outer area is at the S.W. and N., to the inner at the N. only. There is said to be a small mound in the centre of the camp, but it is hard to find for the heather.

The series of enclosures round the camp is probably of later date. There is *a magnificent view* from this point. I must quote Mr. Allcroft's estimate of this place (*Earthwork of England*, p. 118). 'The camp itself is so perfect, so regular, so *mignon*, that it is positively a thing of beauty in its very design . . . The effect is nothing less than charming, and quite unlike that afforded by any other camp . . . As a thing to gaze upon, Old Burrow would be delightful anywhere, and set amidst such surroundings it is a revelation'.

BELL'S POCKET GUIDE TO DEVON (1929)

The vanished age of leisure (for the gentry that is) is here recaptured by the Revd Thornton, whose recollections cover almost exactly the period of greatest change on Exmoor. He knew the Knights and the moor before they began their improvements, and Glenthorne he remembers with great affection for its open-house hospitality and the friends he met there:

I was continually at Glenthorne. At all hours of the night my poor pony was traversing either the lower path through Ashley Lodge and Culbone Wood, or the lane through the farms above, or the high road by Hurlstone Rocks. Mr. Halliday was kindness itself, and an old friend of the Thornton family. He was the son of a Scotch doctor, who in company with a friend named Farquhar (head of the Farquhar family) had gone out to India in the days of Warren Hastings, when the Pagoda tree still grew to be shaken. He was in deacon's orders, and had become known to our family when acting as curate in the Isle of Wight. On the death of his father and of an elder brother he had acquired much property, married a Scotch lady named Gardiner, dropped his profession, purchased the parish of

Countesbury, and built Glenthorne. He was a very remarkable man, of shy and retiring habits, very plain, with a marvellous play of countenance, full of wit and anecdote, a great traveller, and very hospitable. Mrs. Halliday was always kind, and I had the run of the house. . . .

To Glenthorne also came the Knights from Simonsbath—Frederic, Charles, and Lewis,—and there I made their acquaintance. Sir Frederic still survives,★ and it is necessary to be careful, but I will venture to say that for wild and reckless daring I have never known the equals of that triumvirate. Age may by that time have cooled them a little, but if they were cool when I first knew them, what must they have been at an earlier date, ere the eldest had married and entered Parliament; the second been much crippled by a fall in the Roman Campagna; and the third tossed nine times by a buffalo cow in the depths of remotest Abyssinia!

The Hallidays had no children of their own, but their house used to be well filled with young people, more especially in the summer, when Lady Cosway (born Halliday) was wont to bring down her four daughters from Cowes, and the two Miss Moresbys would be there. The supply of rough ponies was apparently inexhaustible, and the young pupils from Selworthy, ten miles away, frequently assisted the ladies to explore the whole wild Exmoor Forest, and other places besides.

REMINISCENCES AND REFLECTIONS OF AN OLD WEST COUNTRY CLERGYMAN,
REVD WM H. THORNTON (1899)

In the days before the First World War it was the custom for wealthy families to rent a large house for the summer. The owner would walk out leaving a fully furnished house with servants, gardeners, horses, carriages, grooms, etc. for the new tenant, who would simply move in and carry on, usually becoming part of the social scene as well.

Gladys Lye was thirteen when her family rented Glenthorne for the autumn of 1904, and she kept a diary of her stay. It provides an interesting

★ Sir Frederic Knight died in May, 1897

piece of social history, detailing not only how they spent their days, but also a description of the rooms of the house and how they were furnished, and of the number of staff left to look after the household:

We had two horses, Daisy one half and Bobby the other half of the time. Our Coachman's name was Bale. Prince (a dog) lived in the stable. We had four servants beside Mrs Winders (the housekeeper), Este and Annie in the kitchen and Norman and Beezley, house-maids.

Holidays were leisurely affairs in those days – but then so was life in general if you were wealthy enough. A typical entry reads:

Thursday morning was fairly fine. We did nothing much. Uncle Hubert went shooting, and Ernie and I threw bottles into the sea and shot at them. After lunch some of us drove to County Gate, then walked down picking wortle berries on the way. After dinner Uncle Edward read Lorna Doone, then prayers, then bed.

Excursions took them to Lynton, the Doone Valley and Oare, and there were many walks over the moor. The family also watched the hunt on several occasions:

Wednesday morning was fairly fine. Some of us started early to a meet, Uncle Walter had hired a pretty little horse. I was rather slow at the meet, and it began to rain about twelve o'clock, at last we drove home. When we had been home about ten minutes the master and a lot of horsemen rode past the front door and up to the wood at the back of the gardener's house, then nothing much happened but solitary dogs kept wandering round the garden and one dog stole a leg of mutton. Then a lot of men and dogs and the master went across the little meadow. We followed them along the cliff then came back and on to the beach.

The Stag was in the water and they decided to follow it along the beach, Eric and I went a little way then went up the little path, we

met Uncle Walter at the top and watched the hunters from the cliff. The huntsmen had to leave the stag because it was getting dark and went home.

At the back of the diary, among newspaper clippings concerning the Halliday family and Glenthorne, is this tongue-in-cheek advertisement, written by Uncle Hubert after his visit. The family lived at Leagrave Hall near Luton:

North Devon Coast (In an exquisite position amidst rugged coast scenery with fine views.)
TO BE LET for the autumn or term of years, with a beach of large slippery stones, and 3,000,000 acres of very rough shooting (Baron Leagrave's party, lately in residence, having on October the 1st bagged one partridge). The above delightfully situated residence with lovely grounds and surrounding meadows and woodland of 180 acres. The approach to the house is over three miles of precipes.
The contents of the house are somewhat fly-blown and mouldy, the whole establishment is well suited to a teetotal family and includes a spacious cellar well stocked with empty wine bottles.
Church, village and post office will be found in a neighbouring county, but by arrangement on Sunday evenings, at 7 o'clock in the Dining Room the Revd Dry-as-dust Lye D.D. will read a sermon on 'Is life worth living?' or other subject. For testimonials and full particulars apply to Mr Hubert Blundell, Ribbon Department, Cheapside, Luton.

Culbone drew various emotions from its visitors. Most found it romantic, and one or two felt moved to expound at great lengths on the 'murmuring ocean', 'billowing trees' and 'Almighty presence':

The church is the picture of seclusion and quiet, and appears on the first view as a place admirably adapted for religious worship, to receive the fervent throbbings of man crying for mercy to his Creator: the impressive grandeur of the surrounding hills, by a

GLENTHORN, ON THE COUNTY BORDER, HOME OF THE HALLIDAY FAMILY

STAFF PHOTOGRAPH

natural transition, raises the mind to the Power that produced them; and our admiration and reverence are followed by the most animating views of the intentions of Providence, from the analogy of the adaptation in every part of the creation of the means to some wise end. But it is rather too poetical a situation for the general mixture of a common congregation; besides, men who are wearied with the toils of the week, require, on the seventh day, some repose; and to those who live on the heights or downs, the descent to Culbone is far from a relaxation of labour; the fatigue of the body will abate the pious fervour of the mind, and a state of lukewarm devotion must in consequence too often prevail.

PICTURESQUE EXCURSIONS IN DEVONSHIRE AND CORNWALL, T.H. WILLIAMS AND T. JOHNS (1804)

This spot is as truly romantick as any perhaps which the kingdom can exhibit. The magnitude, height, and grandeur of the hills, rocks, and woods, at the back and on each side of the cove; the solemnity of the surrounding scene, the sound of the rivulet roaring down its craggy channel; the steep impassable descent from the church down to the beach; the dashing of the waves on a rough and stony shore at an awful distance below; the extent of the channel, and finely varied coast and mountains of Wales beyond it; form a scene peculiarly adapted to strike the mind with pleasure and astonishment.

This parish cannot be approached on horseback without great difficulty, and even danger; the road from Porlock being only a path about two feet wide, winding in a zigzag direction along the slope of the hills, and often interrupted by large loose stones and roots of trees. The woods abound with whortleberries, and a variety of fine polypodies, lichen, and other mosses; among which is some of the yellow rein-deer moss, very bright and scarce. There are also some rare plants; and many wild deer, foxes, badgers, and martin cats, inhabit these woods.

During the three winter months the fun is never seen here; being entirely hid by the height of the surrounding hills.

HISTORY AND ANTIQUITIES OF SOMERSET, REVD J. COLLINSON (1791)

CULBONE CHURCH

The Charcoal Burners of Culbone

My wanderings through the Culbone Woods over the last 50 years have enabled me to trace the work of the charcoal burners who used to live there. The last man who remembered them was 80 years old when I talked to him some 20 years ago; the last burnings must have taken place a hundred years back. He remembered the pits vividly, and some of the burners, because from an early age he used to accompany his people through the woods on their way to sell fish at Glenthorne.

According to the tales I have heard, the old inhabitants of Porlock Weir had always been told by their fathers and forefathers that the original charcoal burners were a colony of Lepers. These people lived and worked in the woods until they died. I always understood that they were not permitted to cross over to the Porlock side of Culbone water, and that a lepers' window was built into one side of Culbone Church, so that they could participate in the worship there.

The only pits I have examined were all between Culbone and Glenthorne. There are many of them, well-preserved, and still containing useable charcoal. This was of very good quality and would

PORLOCK HIGH STREET

would have been easily roofed by flat stones and branches.

The pits are always near roughly made paths and tracks, now mostly overgrown. These tracks had probably been made for the transport of the charcoal by pannier donkeys or small ponies. These beasts must have been led, with their loads, to places where the charcoal could be exchanged for necessities such as grain, flour, salt, fish, flint, and roughly-made tools.

Meat could have presented no difficulty at all, because until the last one was killed some 60 years ago, a huge flock of feral goats roamed the woods. These goats could have solved the problem of milk supply, since in the old days milk was a very scarce item. I have heard the old people of Porlock talk of there being only two sources of milk for many years, one at Bossington and the other at Yarner. An old path leading from the Weir up to Yarner was called 'the milk road.' Then, of course, there were deer, rabbits, birds of a sort, a few hares and sheep at times.

I have always thought that some of the very old paths which lead down the cliffs to the beach might have been made to enable the burners to meet boats inshore, dispose of their charcoal, receive payment in kind, and perhaps for them to fish. Later, smugglers may have used these paths for their own purposes.

EXMOOR REVIEW, 'AFGHAN OF PORLOCK' (1962)

have been easily marketed whilst fresh, and probably much sought after. These pits were never very far from the small freshets which cascade down to the sea, and one can sometimes discover small stone ruins, probably the remnants of roughly constructed huts which

FIVE

Smugglers All

Much smuggling took place all along this coast in the brave days of old, but it seems to have died out about the year 1870.

Cargoes were run at Heddons Mouth, Woody Bay, Lee, and Lynton, the luggers coming in at high tide and pitching their cargo overboard. Then, at low water on a dark evening would come the ponies, each well clipped, hogged and docked, and even soaped to escape capture; then the barrels would be slung on crooks across their backs, four to each pony, but only two if there were a rider. Away would move the string in Indian file through the night on the road to Bristol or Exeter, until some well-known trysting place was reached where the load was temporarily cached to be picked up and taken on by yet another file. Such a stage there was at a point on the Barnstaple-Exeter road, where stood and still stands a certain crooked oak, which is a well-known fixture for hounds.

One old man seemed to think that if the barrels were neither being moved or distributed they could not be touched, but I fancy the gauger would have had a word or two to say about that.

At any rate another old man informed me that on one occasion fifty barrels of spirits were hidden away near an old cottage in the Parracombe Valley and in fact were covered up by a stack of turves. The excisemen got wind of this, and turning up at the house in force proceeded to make a thorough search.

The owner of the cottage recognising that prompt action was necessary, jumped on to his turf-stack where he started throwing down the turves as fast as he could. Some of them hit the excisemen and the air was full of dust and flying turves. Smaller and smaller grew the stack.

At last the Revenue men got tired of the business and ordered the man to stop, for they argued that there could be nothing underneath as otherwise he would not have been so ready to pull it all to pieces. And off they went leaving the barrels undisturbed when another five minutes would have revealed the secret! . . .

Everyone knew about it; everyone was in it; the squire looked the other way and the parson went to bed leaving his stable-door unlocked, at which times his pony would be found mysteriously missing for that night, whilst its place in the stall would be usurped by an anker of the right Nantes.

The old people with whom I have talked on this subject all seemed very unrepentant and some expressed the wish that the old days might come again.

EXMOOR, W. SHERRACOMBE (1920)

With its long and difficult coastline, its proximity to Ireland and its remoteness from the long arm of the law, it was inevitable that Exmoor should have its fair share of smugglers. Those hidden bays, long and empty miles of cliff, wooded valleys, and remote farmsteads and cottages must have made the North Devon and Somerset coast a nightmare for the overstretched preventive and customs men. For many decades the smugglers had Exmoor to themselves and smuggling was looked upon as acceptable, the only crime was being caught, and even then the local population was on your side and probably even the local magistrates, so that conviction was most unlikely and escape more of a certainty:

Something has to be written of the smugglers of the West. In earlier days all classes of society were disposed to regard evasions of revenue laws as venial and anything but criminal. The men who were

WOODY BAY, LYNTON

successful in running a cargo found no difficulty whatever in disposing of it. If merchants were not always accessible, the country gentry had no objection to the flavour of the brandy that had paid no duty, and slept no less comfortably because the sheets of Irish linen had escaped the king's officers. Smuggling must have been comparatively easy in our district, and there is abundant reason for saying that the trade flourished. With easy access from the sea to a country that could not be adequately patrolled, even if patrolling had been well organized, which it was not, with every facility for concealment, the 'fair-trader' had everything in his favour.

The earliest historical document known to me which bears upon this subject is the report of William Culliforde, who was Surveyor-General of Customs to Charles II. In 1682 he was on a visit of inquiry in our neighbourhood. Evidently there had been trouble with the revenue officers, who were suspected of connivance with the smugglers, and Culliforde was in the country to set matters straight. He made full investigation at the ports, and the results of his inquiry are given in the voluminous reports sent by him to London. A few extracts—I have not space for more—will be found instructive. . . .

Culliforde has much complaint to make of Minehead. He suspended James Hellier the 'Tydsman' there, and prayed that he might be dismissed,

He being notoriously guilty, yet a very cunning fellow and hath ruled and governd the Port many years to his majestys prejudice. Henry Clement the other Tydsman, who is a Baliffe and keeps an alehouse, I had severall times upon examinacion and in the presence of Mr Sandys the collector and Mr William Macey he confessed severall frauds and miscarryages in the said Port, but before I had leisure to take his information he was prevailed on to deny the same upon assurance from Coll. Lutterall (as I have been informed) that he shall still be continued his employment. . . .

On the 13th June, 1682, Mr. Culliforde says,

I went to visit Porlock, which is about four miles from Mynehead where there is a very deep Bay & a good Harbour for small Vessels,

OLD COTTAGES, ALCOMBE, MINEHEAD

to which place there are severall that belong, which trade over sea. The officer Richard Davis is an active young fellow, hath hitherto been paid £5 per Ann. by incidents; he very well deserves £10 per Ann. and be established, it being a place of Trade and where great quantities of Herrings are taken and cured, which begets a great concourse of people and small craft, that may be of dangerous consequence to the Customes unlesse well guarded.

This last extract is important. In a few lines it tells us a great deal of Porlock and its trade after the Restoration.

Enough has been extracted from this interesting report to show the extent of unlawful trade in our neighbourhood, and the audacity with which it was carried on. . . .

Once landed the cargoes were carried inland for distribution as speedily as possible. But temporary hiding-places were none the less necessary. There were plenty about Porlock. There was one at lonely Bromhan, under the floor of the barn. One day it became necessary to relay the floor, which had opened at the joints. A great-uncle of Mr. James Huish, of Parson's Street, was taken into the secret, and undertook to do the work in one day, and did it. In return he was to be treated as a favoured customer. He was well entertained, got out of his road going home, fell into the Water, and suffered from gout ever after. In Higher Doverhay farmhouse there was another such place, contrived between an inner and outer wall. A second wall had been built outside the main wall of the house at the dairy end. The thatched roof was brought down to cover the space between the two. The new wall therefore looked from the outside like the main wall of the house. The hold was approached from the dairy through a small opening, which could be concealed by placing a milk pan before it. When discovered a few years ago, during the progress of alterations, the stands for the spirit kegs were still in place. At West Porlock there was a hiding-place in the cottage next to, and westward of the forge. There also, at the cottage formerly the ancient chapel, was another place of concealment under a cow-house.

Another was discovered in a curious way. About fifty years ago, as

BOSSINGTON VILLAGE

I was told by one still living who was present at the time, a hunted hare disappeared below ground in one of the small inclosures which then made up the large field of to-day between Poole's wood and the Bossington lane. By digging, the hole was made large enough for a man to enter. He found a chamber nine or ten feet square, and rather over a man's height. I was not told whether the sides were lined in any way, or how the roof was supported. The plough had passed over it for many a year. Some of the hounds were handed down, and the hare killed. This hiding-place, which was very convenient for a landing on the most secluded part of the beach, was placed about two-thirds of the distance from the gate near the junction of Old lane and the Bossington lane towards Poole's wood.

HISTORY OF PART OF WEST SOMERSET, C. CHADWYCK HEALEY (1901)

A lighter note comes from Richard Jefferies:

There is a story of the smugglers—once notorious folk on these hills—teaching their horses to understand the usual words of command backwards. If they were driving pack-horses along at night with a load of brandy landed from a lugger, and were met by the revenue man, who ordered them to stop that the packs might be searched, the smugglers, like good and loyal subjects, called 'Whoa! whoa!' Instantly the horses set off at a tearing gallop for they understood 'Whoa,' as 'Gee-up.'

'SUMMER IN SOMERSET', RICHARD JEFFERIES (1887)

But there was another side to seafaring folk, amply demonstrated in this stirring account of shipwreck and rescue recounted by the Revd Thornton. Any rescues at sea depended upon a brave crew of local fishermen volunteering to row through seas which would normally keep all sane men in port. It is a miracle that anyone was saved at all:

The next winter, the famous Crimean winter of 1854–5, was even colder than the last. The severe weather did not set in until after Christmas, and then its severity was appalling. Our poor soldiers suffered terribly in the Crimea, and the season brought me an adventure or two which I have not forgotten, and which I never shall forget.

I was sitting in my room one stormy morning, when a great cry was raised in the street, and I was told that there was a wreck in the bay. I hurried out under shelter of the low wall of the pier, and my heart grew sick within me as I saw a small vessel come round the rocks from the westward. She was about half a mile from land, her two masts were broken short off, and four human beings were lashed to their stumps. The top hamper was clinging to her side and causing her to heel over to leeward. A strong sea was running, with the current up channel, and two miles in front loomed the gigantic mass of the North Foreland, stretching far across the head of the bay. White foam was flecking its steep and murderous sides well nigh to the summit, one thousand two hundred feet above. One thing was manifest. No one could doubt the doom of crew and of vessel when those two short miles should have been traversed. Lynmouth at this time possessed no life-boat, but many stout, broad-bottomed boats were in the river, or hard by on the shore.

The coastguard lieutenant, Hodges by name, . . . was in bed with low fever, and I was sick with impotent benevolence. Presently from out of his bed, looking pale, but dressed very smartly, came the lieutenant and called for a crew. Eight men volunteered and stepped into a boat, as, also, did Mr. Hodges, with the tiller in his hand. The men shewed no signs of excitement, they were only rather more grumpy in their manner than usual, for they meant to risk their lives, and to do so with as little civility as possible, after the fashion of true-born Englishmen. There was no kissing of wives, no hugging of children, no hand-shaking with friends.

'Now men, get into the boat, can't you?' from Hodges.

'No cause for you to be in such a darned hurry, neither,' for reply; and then 'Shove her off, and never mind those blazing fools on the bank above you,' as away they went to sea. I shall never, never forget how that boat looked when the first wave caught her as she left the partial shelter of the pier. She stood up like a horse, and I thought she was gone, and all nine with her, but she righted, and the men pulled strong. Often we could not see anything of her in the trough of the waves, and then she would rise and ride over some great rolling pillow of water, only again to disappear. Presently we saw her pass the wreck and come to on the further side. Then she returned, bringing with her two men, one woman, a boy, and a shaggy dog. They were all nearly dead, for they had been drifting for a long time, and the human beings had been lashed to the masts and continually water washed. Then Lieutenant Hodges took off his wet clothes and went to bed to finish his fever comfortably. Dear old fellow, he was living a year or two ago, and for my part I could wish him immortal.

REMINISCENCES AND REFLECTIONS OF AN OLD WEST COUNTRY CLERGYMAN, REVD WM H. THORNTON (1899)

SIX

Porlock Vale

Porlock comes in for almost as much fulsome praise as Lynmouth, although it has never become quite as popular with tourists as Lynmouth. In 1918 it was still full of old world charm, and even today the view as one looks out over the vale and the bay is hard to beat.

> Porlock, thy verdant vale so fair to sight,
> Thy lofty hills, which fern and furze embrown,
> Thy waters, that roll musically down
> Thy woody glens, the traveller with delight
> Recalls to memory.
>
> SOUTHEY

The orchards described by John Presland that were such a feature have almost all disappeared. It appears from old records that there were orchards at Porlock in the days of Elizabeth I. Perhaps they may yet reappear at Porlock so that we, too, may see the 'sweep of blossom, the foam of cherry and pear':

To me Porlock is one of the most beautiful spots in all England. It lies in a green bay—what *was* a bay eight centuries ago—between two towering headlands. On three sides of it rise the heights of Exmoor, barren, beautiful, and windswept; before it stretch the lands over which the Danes sailed, running out to a thin strip of marshland, and then a silvery flat beach, and then the tremulous silver curve of the sea, not like the line of wave that breaks at the foot of cliffs, but a true marshland sea, seeming to come from nowhere, infinitely smooth and faint and distant from the level shore to the dim horizon.

There are many kinds of beauty in the world: beauty of hot suns and delicate mists, of sea and shore, mountain and lake and city; there is the beauty of barren moors and of green orchards, and of flat fertile marshlands where streams run amid a luxuriance of tangled growth, kingcups and meadowsweet and loose-strife and forget-me-nots, and feathery willows and rushes where the reed-warblers sing. And at Porlock there is such a gathering up of these different beauties that it is difficult to describe the pleasure that one has in it. I have told you how it is fenced by Exmoor, and lies within sight of Dunkery Beacon, the highest point of the moors; but it is impossible to convey adequately the peculiar beauty of those great smooth dipping curves, the satisfying breadth and harmony of their line, the way the sunlight lies upon them, and the rich deep shadows that slide into their folds. And below, round Porlock, lie the orchards. I came there once in the spring, and as we turned the last angle of the stony road I saw before me such a sweep of blossom, such a foam of cherry and pear, white above the luxuriant grass, and of that delicate flushed rose of the apple-blossom, so exquisite a range of green, the hazy green of willows and the bright clear green of hawthorn, that it seemed impossible it should lie just under those miles on miles of moor where nothing bloomed but furze and heather.

The green fields that stretched away to the sea were just such fields as in the 'Romaunt of the Rose' or the poems of the troubadours, fields verdantly green, and starred with daisies and golden with buttercups—the 'enamelled meads' of Chaucer and the little illumined pictures of the fourteenth-century manuscripts; and the hedges were just such hedges, incredibly green, with here and there a break for the misty silver of the blackthorn. Wherever flowers could bloom they bloomed, in the gardens, in the hedges by the the roadside, in the crannies in the walls.

LYNTON AND LYNMOUTH, J. PRESLAND (1918)

PORLOCK HILL

In those early days of the motor-car there was still some fun to be had from the struggling motorists coping with the steep gradients of Porlock Hill.

The writer of this delightful piece, poking gentle mockery at travellers in wheeled vehicles, described Exmoor as the 'Riding Playground of England', and he obviously saw Exmoor as one great glorious expanse of countryside devoted to the horse, where any other form of transport was considered an intrusion. The author, Cecil Aldin, was a well known animal artist, especially of dogs appearing in cartoon-like illustrations:

Porlock is full of stables of the hunting, hack, or children's pony variety. Hissing men in baggy riding breeches abound everywhere, and notices of the various hunting and livery stables catch the eye at every corner. The village postmaster who finds you houses and the village tailor who sells sporting pictures and cuts jodhpurs are both men who give visitors information on every conceivable subject, from hotels and rooms to let to ponies and purveyors of food commodities. I have always liked that word 'purveyor.'. . .

Years ago, when the car was not so efficient as it is to-day, Porlock inhabitants would congregate after church, on an August Sunday morning, to see the attempt to climb the dread Porlock Hill. At that time, before the new Toll Road was completed, the grand-stand on Sunday morning for this hill-climbing exhibition was at the first sharp bend some 300 yards above the Ship Inn, and at the point where the motor driver first sees the 1 in 4 gradient he has in front of him before he can continue his journey to Lynton.

The bank on each side of the roadway used to be lined with the expectant faces of the 'city fathers' as the hoot and honk of the arriving car was heard on its way to the corner. The best effects were produced when a car arrived loaded up with paterfamilias, wife and often uncles, aunts and children. The expression on the face of the driver as he came round the bend was always rewarded by a round of applause—certainly a 'smile'—from the waiting audience, and the fun began when he immediately attempted to rush the hill with a radiator often nearly boiling from a long journey. In most cases the man at the wheel would completely lose his head, muddle his gears, forget where his brake-handle was, and trickle backwards after only accomplishing a few yards. Luggage, wife, aunts, uncles and children would be left stranded with one wheel against the bank unless the active A.A. man jumped on the footboard and clasped the wheel, so steering the car backward into comparative safety. From daily practice he had become an expert at this on every type of car.

Sometimes a car would reach that bend 300 yards above without its bottom gear failing to accomplish the climb, but in very few cases, in the comparatively early days of the modern motor car, was Porlock Hill climbed without a pause and human-power help.

Since then I have always used the Toll Road, for on the first three occasions on which I saw a car on Porlock Hill number one was only a charred chassis burnt out at the top; number two was upside down at the bottom through running backwards when out of control, and the third belonged to an American, and was gaily burning half-way down, the driver having attempted to come down on his brakes alone without changing down. After these incidents the Toll

Road, which starts a few yards above the Old Ship Inn and comes out on the top of Hawkcombe Head on the Lynton road, was for me.

EXMOOR: THE RIDING PLAYGROUND OF ENGLAND, CECIL ALDIN (1935)

Mr Aldin would have found himself more at home in the days recalled in this piece when Porlock, 'a quaint old place wakes several times daily to the inspiriting sound of the horn of coaches . . .'

Nowadays it is a different kind of coach and a different, less melodic horn that disturbs the slumbers of Porlock, though the village has long since been rudely awoken by the pressures of twentieth-century traffic, passing with great difficulty through its narrow main street:

A long straggling street, with curious old-fashioned cottages, many with tall round chimneys, instead of windows, facing the street, a protection, says Savage, against spies in the troublous times of the Stuarts, a profusion of flowers wherever flowers will grow, such is the ancient town of Porlock. Behind, steep wooded hills tower moorwards towards the range of Dunkery, while seawards, a flat stretch of fertile land intervening, the rugged headland of Bossington or Hurlstone Point pushes itself into the waters of the Channel. In summer the quaint old place wakes several times daily to the inspiriting sound of the horn of coaches bearing names that remind one forcibly of *Lorna Doone* and *Katerfelto*; in winter it is the quietest of the quiet. Of Porlock in winter, as of Chagford, on the outskirts of Dartmoor, little can be said. It is reported that a traveller, approaching the latter and asking its name, was met by a doleful shake of the head, and the melancholy exclamation 'Chaggiford – O Lord!' From November to May the town under Exmoor is almost as shut out from the world as the old Stannary town beneath the shadow of Darmoor.

But in the days of Saxon rule, . . . it was quite a famous place. Here was a palace of their kings, and on the hills yonder a chace, where they not only hunted the red deer, but wolves as well. In an earlier part of this work we have alluded to the Lidwiccas' invasion of 918, when an attempt was made to land here, but the assailants were

THE SHIP INN, PORLOCK

beaten off, as well as to the more serious raid of the following century, when Harold descended upon Porlock, only to find his countrymen rise against him, and that a bloody fight was necessary.

In the end the sons of Godwin triumphed, and, sailing away laden with spoil, they joined their father, and, returning in force to London, the haughty Earl was pardoned, King Edward making a virtue of necessity. In a wood, rather more than a mile south of the church, the remains of a small oval camp mark, it is supposed, the earthwork thrown up by the invaders.

In ancient days there is some probability that Porlock was a sea-port, and that, as was the case with Glastonbury,

> The flood of the Severn sea
> Flowed over half the plain.

According to most writers the name is derived from the Anglo-Saxon *Port*, a harbour, and *luc* or *lucan*, to shut up—the enclosed port. It is scarcely necessary to state that no harbour exists there now. The sea has retired, and Porlock Weir, two miles distant, is the port of Porlock.

The Parish Church, dedicated to Saint Dubritius, is a structure of fair proportions, though not altogether beautiful to the eye. It is spoilt, in fact, by an amazingly hideous truncated spire covered with tiles. This spire, which is octagonal, once rose to a considerable height, but was destroyed by a storm in 1700.

EXMOOR, J.L.W. PAGE (1890)

The architecture, including the chimneys, also drew comment from the Reverend Warner:

An odd effect is produced by the very unusual stile of architecture, in which the houses are, for the most part, built; for here, as in other small country places distant from the seat of the arts, one model is generally followed in constructing the dwellings of their inhabitants. At Porlock they rise to the height of two stories, and are mostly thatched; but the fashion of that place has determined, that the chimnies instead of preserving their usual retired situation, should be formed in the front of the houses, and their backs project into the street.

WALKS THROUGH WALES AND THE WESTERN COUNTIES,
REVD R. WARNER (1799)

Porlock Bay has undergone considerable changes over the centuries and is changing still. No one knows how long it will be before the sea once again flows over the low-lying fields to reach the edge of the little town. Mr Chadwyck Healey moved on to Porlock Weir and the Bay, quoting from Leland:

The ceaseless movement of the sea during the long procession of centuries has worked a marked change in places. In front of the stony beach at Porlock and at Minehead—the 'chesil' of the old records—are still to be seen between high and low water marks the semi-fossilized remains of what was once a forest of large trees. The marsh lands of Porlock were formerly covered in the whole by the sea. As time rolled on the waters left them, but there is reason to believe that as late as the fourteenth century the sea formed a creek, or haven, like the Hawn at Dunster, where nowadays in wet seasons the water lies in a wide shallow pool. This was no doubt 'le Lake' mentioned in the extent taken after the death of Simon de Roges. In this water probably swam the cygnets that were captured for Lady Harington. The great beach has changed all this. Constantly moving, heaping itself high above the low lands, encroaching here and there upon the grazing ground, it still protects the marshes. Open a breach through the huge mound and a large part of the low-lying land below the town would be submerged. Leland, who was in Somerset in 1540–42, does not tell us much about the district. All he says of Porlock is that the 'rode that is communely callid Porlogh Bay is a meatly good rode for shippes.' From Culbone to Stert he says, 'moste parte of the shore is hilly ground and nere the shore is no store of wood: that that is ys al in hegge rowes of enclosures. There is great

RATTLING THROUGH PORLOCK VILLAGE

plenty of benes in this quarter and great plenty of whete and catelle.' Gerard, who wrote nearly a hundred years later of Porlock, says: 'This is still a slender harbour and over it stands the towne which surely I cannott commend. Nott farre from which you may see an antient mannor house for the lords of it neighboured with a parke and chase, who enjoy divers priviledges and great royalties for fishinge.' Gerard may have had in his mind the 'slender harbour' at Porlock weir, which was then in existence . . . , but his description otherwise well fits what might then have been left of the ancient creek. We see from Leland's chance allusion to the absence of wood except in hedgerows, that the large common fields of earlier times had already been inclosed. The latter half of the nineteenth century has seen a great diminution of timber in the vale, as even men of middle age can testify. In 1807 a visitor wrote: 'From Lynch over a flat opening to Porlock Bay, consisting of most fertile land in small inclosures with richly wooded hedgerows, to the village of Porlock.' Most of this timber has gone, but, for compensation, we have the beautiful woods of Selworthy, planted early in this century by Sir Thomas Dyke Acland.

HISTORY OF PARTS OF WEST SOMERSET, C. CHADWYCK HEALEY (1901)

Here, with the last word on Porlock, is Cecil Aldin again. He recalls the great days of the Anchor Hotel at Porlock Weir and gives what must surely be a unique account of a unique sport – the hunting of the wasp!:

The Anchor Hotel at Porlock Weir is the most enjoyable of all. I do hope that it still keeps the honoured remains of the pair-horse 'Anchor Bus' in which so many of us first wearily travelled to the Weir from Minehead station. When I last stayed there it was holding itself bravely together under a hedge between Worthy Manor and the inn. Here for 25 years it had stayed waiting for burial.

The 'Anchor Hotel' could still be traced on each side of the conveyance that was once the pride of old John Goddard's heart, the apple of his eye and the only pair-horse bus that travelled from Porlock to Minehead; the only private omnibus of a great hunting hotel of the period.

I once painted a fox and hounds on coach panels for a friend. I wish, in the new days of his omnibus, I had known John Goddard better and had been allowed to paint a 'warrantable' stag upon its door behind, for I think he would have liked to have seen it as his bus gaily drove away from the hotel porch to meet his hunting visitors.

A hotel-keeper he was, but first of all a great sportsman, a character and a staghunter. The exigencies of the hotel business he would never allow to interfere with his sporting fixtures of private likes or dislikes, and if he did not take to you, or the look of you, as a guest, he told you so very plainly.

John Fothergill of the 'Spread Eagle' at Thame was a polished courtier compared to John Goddard of the Anchor Inn, Porlock Weir—if you were not to his taste!

There were two things I always loved about John and his house. The first was his one and only bathroom, and the rush home we all had to get in first on hunting days. The second his delightful habit (by which he could soon starve out an unpleasant visitor) of carving all the joints himself, and always, before doing so, asking exactly for whom he was carving, that he might give his guests the quantity and quality they fancied; and what he lost on the roundabouts he could make up on the swings. If any of the guests did not run smoothly on his hotel-lines, they would always be served last and least, if it became necessary to remove them by fair means or foul.

I have called the Anchor a great hunting inn, and so it was, but not in size, for it only had about ten or twelve bedrooms, one bath, three private sitting-rooms and enormous stabling. The visitors' book for the stag-hunting season showed the same names year after year. They seemed to continue coming until they left this world.

If you went once to the Anchor you went always, and from year to year the same bedroom and sitting-room were reserved for each honoured guest. You were just as much a part of the house as the proprietor or the boots and chambermaids. . . .

Every year when I travelled to Porlock it seemed more like 'going home' than anything else, although I had a house in Berkshire and many interests there.

PORLOCK WEIR

That is the charm of one's favourite inn. That welcome of the staff on one's arrival. But at Porlock Weir in those days it was not only the staff of the Anchor, it was all the Perkyns and Pollards, Old 'Villum' and his friends, the habitués of the sea-wall, who grasped you by the hand and gave you welcome. You felt that they had lived through the quiet winter solely for this reunion. They told you about staghunting sport, the fishing season, the conger-eels, the births, deaths and marriages—in fact, all the thrilling news of Porlock town—as you sat on the quay wall. 'Turkey,' as it was called. The derivation of its name we discovered was from the sentence, 'Come on ter quay.' The seats on the quay were, therefore, always known by those in the hotels as Turkey, and there, after dinner, we smoked our evening cigars.

This same little band of sportsmen from all over England forgathered every year from August to October at the hospitable Anchor, and much talk there was on Turkey of fox, stag, otter and other kinds of sport.

It was when at the Weir that we had a plague of wasps and so discovered a sport new to most of us.

It was in the rather early days of the West Somerset Polo Club at Dunster and one of the players kept his ponies at the club, but lived at the Anchor most of the time when play was not possible. He did not hunt the stag, but was an enthusiastic wasp-hunter, and treated the destruction of a few nests as the serious business of each non-polo day. His method of hunting was based on his own scientifically worked-out theory and was most successful for, that season, he took over one hundred nests.

About four o'clock on each day he would take up a position on the low wall in front of the Anchor, a small bottle of some poisonous mixture sticking out of his jacket pocket. To anyone watching he seemed to be gazing vacantly into space, his eyes fixed on points a little above the height of the tallest man.

Suddenly his whole frame would stiffen—his hackles go up, so to speak—and he would rise like a man in a trance to follow a series of glistening yellow bodies and tinsel wings which converged on some wall; house or tree as a vanishing point twenty or thirty yards away.

In such cases he was on a screaming scent and, on reaching the spot where the wasps had vanished, he would again sit and gaze thoughtfully until he located another stage in the wasps' homeward journey, and so on until finally all the straight-flying insects came to one vanishing point, and there was the nest.

At midday and in the evening, as soon as he saw wasps flying in straight lines like city workers travelling home and not swooping about in all directions, he took up positions to draw for homeward-bound wasps. Sometimes he had a long hunt; often he hit off many lines converging in one direction from places two or three hundred yards apart, but when once he could locate two or three lines he was able to discover points—through some building-wall or tree—where they came together in their direct route and would hit the trail again on the far side. In this way he would continue the hunt until the nest was discovered and exterminated.

A zigzagging wasp, when still feeding, had no interest for him. It was not a 'warrantable' wasp until full, but the direct homeward-bound quarry never failed to start him on a hunt and we would presently hear, borne on the still evening air, his shrill 'Who-whoop' of victory.

Anyone can, of course, spot wasps when they are buzzing round their nests, but his art was the trailing of them. By long practice he had become such an expert that he knew to a minute the various times of day when the wasp returned home.

I followed a hunt with him once or twice; I also found it a most exciting pastime, and can thoroughly recommend it as exercise for old or young. The 'Who-whoop' that my friend gave out when he finally marked to ground, and produced his poison gas, could be heard all over Porlock Weir, and everyone would rush out to be in at the kill.

A funny combination this enthusiasm for the game of polo and the sport of wasp-hunting!

EXMOOR: THE RIDING PLAYGROUND OF ENGLAND, CECIL ALDIN (1935)

SEVEN

And on to Minehead

'The Romance of Peasant Life' was the title of an article that appeared in THE MORNING ADVERTISER in July 1873. The writer, Mr Heath, gives a vivid picture of the painful contrast presented by the peasant's outward aspect of the cottages in a certain neighbouring hamlet (Mr Heath was writing from Porlock) with their miserable interiors.

Another turning, this time round to the left, after a few steps up the lane, and a most charming sight met my view. Straight in front a narrow path led up under a kind of vista. On my right hand there was a line of creeper-bound cottages. There were 18 in all. Facing the cottages was a row of little gardens, overshadowed by fruit trees. Here and there rustic beehives were scattered over these gardens which contained flowers and shrubs in addition to their little crops of vegetables. The walls of some of the cottages were almost hidden by the plants and shrubs which trailed upon them. This little 'nook' was shut in on almost every side by orchards. . . .

> From glowing orchards forth they peep
> Each from its nook of leaves,
> And fearless there the lowly sleep
> As the birds beneath the eaves.

The lowly sleep . . . Wait a bit. The 'lowly' human element was not wanting. I catch sight of a child without shoes sitting on a doorstep. It was that of No 1 in the row. I went up the steps, knocked at the door and was asked 'Would I please to walk in' by a woman who, with a baby in her arms, stood up on the stone floor as I entered and curtseyed after the custom of the country on catching sight of me. I sat on a chair where I was politely invited to seat myself, and looked around. O God, what a change! Was it possible that man's inhuman selfishness could fill this 'smiling cottage home' with such ignorant, wretched starving human creatures? A piteous tale was unfolded in response to my numerous inquiries. The husband was a carter, and as the wages had been 'risen' during the last few months he was then in receipt of the splendid income of 10s a week, in addition to which he had three pints of cider daily when driving the horses for ordinary work and an extra pint daily when ploughing. No cottage rent given, no 'privileges'. The cottage had the tiny bit of garden-ground, 15 yards—in front, and there was the 'privilege' of paying 7s 9d a year for thirty yards of potato ground. The cottage-rent under the old squire had been £2 2s, but the new squire had raised it to £3 5s. In addition to this, out of his miserable wages this poor creature had to pay 10s a year for rates viz. poor rates, school rates and gas rate for the parish of Minehead. The poor people wondered rightly enough why they had to pay a gas rate when there was no gas within more than a mile of them. Deducting these items of expenditure from the grand total of 10s there was left the magnificent sum of 8s 7d on which to luxuriate each week. In this family there were the husband, his wife and five children, besides the husband's mother, a poor old bedridden women 93 years of age. The eldest of the children was a boy 9½ years of age. This 'ancient' little fellow had commenced his career as a farm labourer, in other words had joined the ranks of a 'bold peasantry, our country's pride' at the age of eight. His wages was then 4d a day, and a pint of cider.

ALLERFORD

Last Lady-day however, his master, perhaps in dread of Joseph Archer or the other 'agitators who cannot let the poor farmers alone' had raised our little hero's wages to 5d a day.

THE *MORNING ADVERTISER*, HEATH (1873)

Richard Jefferies was a tragic figure. Ill health accompanied him all his short life, and caused misunderstanding in his childhood and younger days. Born into a farming community, the weakling lad with the vivid imagination was always a misfit, the pen being no substitute for the plough. Jefferies persisted and his skills were recognized.

His essays on country life and characters remain timeless cameos all too rarely read these days, yet his perception and beautiful prose deserve a wider public and greater acclaim. Henry Williamson regarded him as his own alter ego and described him as 'a genius, a visionary whose thought and feeling were wide as the human world, prophet of an age not yet come into being – the age of sun, of harmony':

Selworthy woods were still in the afternoon heat; except for the occasional rustle of a rabbit or of a pheasant, there was no evidence of life; the sound of the sea was faint and soon lost among the ferns. Slowly, very slowly, great Dunkery grew less hard of aspect, shadows drew along at the base, while again the declining sun from time to time sent his beams into valleys till now dark. The thatched house at Holnicote by the foot of Selworthy much interested me; it is one of the last of thatched houses inhabited by a gentleman and landed pro-prietor. Sir Thomas Acland who resides here is a very large owner. Thatch prevails on his estates; thatched cottages, thatched farmhouses, and his thatched mansion. In the coolness of the evening the birds begin to swing and squirrels played across the lawn in front of Holnicote House. Humble bees hummed in the grass and visited the flowers of the holly bushes. Thrushes sang and chaffinches, and, sweetest of all, if simpler in notes, the greenfinches talked and courted in the trees. Two cuckoos called in different directions, wood-pigeons raised their voices in Selworthy Wood, and rooks went over cawing in their deliberate way. In the level meadow from among the tall grasses

and white wild flowering wild parsley a landrail called 'crake, crake' ceaselessly. There was a sense of rest and quiet, and with it joyousness of bird life, such as should be about an English homestead.

'SUMMER IN SOMERSET', RICHARD JEFFERIES (1887)

Dunkery has always had a special significance for the people of the moor. It dominates the eastern skyline, massive, brooding, its bare bald dome reaching to the clouds, its beginnings lost in the deep sunless combes. The summit is much visited, a broad track leading from the road that passes too conveniently close. Its great height has been made use of since time immemorial when fire beacons swiftly spread the news of great events throughout the country:

But we must strike across the moor on the right and head straight for the Beacon, which is crowned by a cairn of stones and the remains of the hearths on which the beacons were piled. The last time a beacon fire blazed here was on the Coronation of King Edward VII.

It is impossible to survey the cairn which surmounts the hill with-out thinking for a moment of the bygone use of the Beacon. John Ridd himself describes Dunkery: 'The Beacon was rushing up in a fiery storm to heaven, and the form of its flame came and went in the folds, and the heavy sky was hovering. All around it was hung with red, deep in twisted columns, and then a giant beard of flame streamed throughout the darkness. The sullen hills were flanked with light, and the valleys chined with shadow, and all the sombrous moors between awoke in furrowed anger.'

RED GUIDE, WARD LOCK (1911)

Cutcombe is an extensive parish, lying eight miles south from Minehead, and twenty-seven northwest from Taunton. The church and most of the houses are situated in a fruitful vale, called *Watercombe*, bounded by very lofty eminences to the north and south. On the western side is *Dunkery*, a very large and high moun-tain, standing in the several parishes of Cutcombe, Luccombe, Wotton-Courtney, Stoke-Pero, and Exford. From the church at

THE HONICOTE ESTATE THATCHER AT LUCCOMBE

Wotton-Courtney the ascent to its summit is three miles, and very steep. Its base is about twelve miles in circumference. The highest part of it is the south southwest, and by an accurate measurement one thousand seven hundred and seventy feet above the sea at high-water mark. To this height it rises in naked sublimity, and is seen at a vast distance both by sea and land; but frequently the top is obscured in clouds. No part is cultivated, but in many places it is covered with whortleberry plants, divers species of erica, and some rare bog and other mosses, with a little grass intermixed.

On the top of this hill is a vast collection of rough loose stones, from one or two hundred pounds in weight each; and among them the ruins of three large fire-hearths, about eight feet square, and built of rough unwrought stones. These fire-places form an equilateral triangle, and in the center is another hearth considerably larger than the rest. At the distance of near a mile, and more than two hundred feet lower, the vestiges of two other hearths are visible, with vast quantities of rough loose disjointed stones scattered round them. These are the remains of those beacons which were formerly erected on this elevated spot, in order to alarm the country in times of civil discord or foreign invasion. Hence the hill to this day retains the name of *Dunkery Beacon*.

As this is the highest mountain in the west of England, it affords so extensive and noble a prospect, as to merit particular description. In a clear day the view extends from the high lands near Plymouth, on the southwest, to the Malvern-Hills in Worcestershire on the north, which are more than two hundred miles distant from each other. On the west and northwest the British Channel, for near one hundred and thirty miles in length, lies under the eye, with the greater part of South-Wales, from Monmouthshire down to Pembrokeshire, rising in a fine amphitheatre beyond it. To the east and south, the greater part of Somersetshire, Dorset, and Devon, with some parts of Hants and Wilts, appear to view. When the air is clear and serene the line which bounds the horizon cannot be less than five hundred miles in circumference, and takes in fifteen counties.

HISTORY AND ANTIQUITIES OF THE COUNTY OF SOMERSET, REVD JOHN COLLINSON (1791)

CUTCOMBE VILLAGERS

The Hills That Spoke

On a winter afternoon in the year 1897 two men were walking slowly to the summit of Doone Beacon. 'Shall 'ee make it?' asked the younger man.

'Don't ask damn fool questions,' came the reply.

'I only meant . . .'

'You meant I'm eighty-eight and ought to be dead.'

When at last they reached the summit, they found a group of villagers gathered beside an unlit bonfire. 'Blow me down,' exclaimed one of the group. ''Tis Granfer Davy. My dear man, you'm past climbing the Beacon, surely?'

'Then how come I've climbed 'en?' retorted the veteran, prodding the faggots with his stick. Then he glanced at the sky. 'Another 'alf-hour,' he reckoned, 'and this yere will be ablaze. Sixty years a Queen, eh? A real diamond jubilee.'

'I can still remember her silver jubilee,' said his companion. ''Twas way back in '62. Lord, Lord, I must be getting older than I thought. Yes,' he repeated, 'I can remember 1862.'

'I,' said the old man, 'can remember 1815.' The group stared, surprised at being astonished by what they had long known. 'I walked up yere with my uncle. Least, I walked 'alfway. T'other 'alf I rode on his shoulder. And when we arrived, the faggots were piled just where they are now, and old Jonas standing guard over 'em, same as someone was guarding all the others.' He waved his stick. 'High Beacon, Windy Point, Gallows Hill, West Tor . . . all waiting to be lit in case he landed.'

'Napoleon,' someone muttered, as though to emphasise the obvious.

'When my uncle was bo'sun in the *Fearless* he'd seen 'em, hundreds of 'em, Boney's barges, lying off the French coast, just waiting till he'd captured the Channel. But he never did. Then as now, we ruled the waves.'

'But . . .'

'But only just. Terrible short o' ships and men we were. Spending our money on everything except defending our money. 'Twas like

the Armada all over again. Some people never seem to learn.' He noticed a hamper on the ground. 'Do I smell ale?'

'Better be quick about it,' his companion warned. 'I can see pa'son and the womenfolk coming up. Ah, and there's pa'son's sister.'

'That woman?' The old man grabbed a mug. 'Her's the most intemperate Temperancer I ever did meet.' The ale was swallowed in three quick gulps. ''Tis strange times we'm living in, when a man can't wet the whistle without someone rams a tract down his throat.'

So the afternoon faded, growing colder and darker. The parson was already saying: 'According to my watch . . .' when a shout went up. 'There 'tis! Windy Point's afire. Stand back now. Let the vicar see all's done shipshape and Queen's Regulations.' Next moment, a red tongue pouted from the faggots, and the flames spread, blotting out the night and the moor and everything except the spectators. Two minutes later and nine miles away, a voice on West Tor cried: 'Look! Doone Beacon! Stand by, lads. Now's the time. God save the Queen!'

On a summer evening in the year 1977 an old man and a small boy were walking slowly to the summit of Doone Beacon. 'Shall 'ee make it?' asked the greybeard.

'Is it far?' came the reply.

'Far enough to give 'ee another ride. But this time granfer's tired, too, so we'll wait till Dad brings the Land Rover.'

'I'm hot, granfer.'

'Better that than cold, like I was when I first came up yere. My mother carried me most o' the way.'

'Didn't 'er 'ave no Land Rover?'

'The only land roving your great-grandmother ever did was on 'er own two feet, or sometimes with old Jonas in his wagon. Now, let's sit down and see if there's any o' they peppermints left.'

Five minutes later the Land Rover appeared, crammed with villagers. 'It's long past his bedtime,' the child's mother complained.

'Get along with 'ee girl,' said the old man. 'This yere's going to be a sight he may never see again. Twenty-five years a Queen. And what years! When they lit the fire for Victoria's jubilee we were the greatest nation in the world. And what are we now?'

'Pack it in, grandpop,' said a voice. 'This is 1977.'

'That's exactly what I was about to say,' the old man replied.

'But I remember it well, that jubilee. Old Jim Davy climbed up, carrying his eighty-eight years like they were no more than a handful o' pebbles. My mother said afterwards he told 'em about Napoleon's bonfire and all the French barges waiting to invade. We'd not enough ships, said Davy, and not enough men. I reckon 'twas the same as Dunkirk in 1940.'

'Did Victoria's bonfire burn good?'

'Bright enough to please Old Nick 'isself. I remember Davy pointing with his stick, counting all the other fires, forty-four on 'em, like red stars from yere to Worcestershire and then across the water to Wales.'

Day was a long time dying, but when the last glow from its pyre had faded, a voice shouted: 'Look there! Windy's alight.'

And a few moments later a voice on West Tor shouted: 'They'm firing Doone. Let's give 'em an answer.'

So they all stood on their hilltop—men and women and children—counting the myriad fires whose flames were like tongues uttering a grateful salutation: 'God save the Queen!'

COUNTRY TALK AGAIN, J.H.B. PEEL (1970)

'In old writings called Lollocksburghe, but who he was should give it that name I know not', wrote Thomas Gerard in 1633. He went on:

So called I should rather deeme from the lowe situation, or Lucombe from the warmnes, which wee yett call Lewe, then from the River Lock if ever it had that name before Hollinshead became Godfather unto it. Whensoever it gott that name, it gave it to the antient Owners of it, who flourished here from before ye date of antient evidence untill Edward ye 2. tyme; when Elizabeth Daughter of Hugh de Luckombe brought Luckombe unto her husband Sir Oliver de St. John of a noble Family, as by his Armes you may per-

ceive. Oliver had Henry, whose Grandchylde and Heire Joane was married to Nicholas Arundell of Trerice in Cornwall, whose successors were lately Owners of Luckombe.

PARTICULAR DESCRIPTION OF THE COUNTY OF SOMERSET, THOMAS GERARD (1900)

Luccombe came in for a particularly detailed scrutiny three centuries later in a book entitled EXMOOR VILLAGE. Just why Luccombe was chosen rather than any other Exmoor village is not made clear, but it gives a fascinating and unique view of village life in the recent past.

The writer would obviously feel at home in any government department today. The statistical details are overwhelming – even including the colours of the internal decorations. What must the villagers have thought of it all?

There are thirty-one houses in and neighbouring the village of Luccombe. Of these sixteen are detached, twelve are semi-detached and three in a row. To anyone visiting the village for the first time, a striking feature is the thatched roofs. It is easy to come away from Luccombe with the impression that most of the cottages are thatched, and this impression is strengthened by the fact that many of the farm buildings in and around the village have thatched roofs. Actually, of the inhabited houses twenty-one have tiled roofs, seven thatched roofs, and three slate roofs. The majority—twenty of the thirty-one—have walls of pale yellow or cream; seven of red stone, two of grey stone, and two of roughcast.

For interior decoration Luccombe people prefer pastel shades of distemper, and twice as many rooms are distempered as are decorated with wall-paper. . . .

What some guests think of Luccombe is found in the comments in prose and verse which they often write in the visitors' book before they leave. At Porch Cottage, Mrs Tame, whose husband is a carter at Blackford farm and who 'does' for old Mrs Lawrence up at Wychanger five days a week from 10.30 A.M. to 3.30 P.M., also manages to take visitors and to give them an excellent reception. The poem in her visitors' book of which she is particularly proud is this one:

I lay upon my comfy bed,
The sun shone through the pane,
A knock came on the door, I said
'Is that you, Mrs Tame?'

She brought me in my cup of tea,
It tasted really good
And this was no-wise odd, because
Somehow I thought it would.

Then I arose and wandered far,
And somtimes got home late,
For she's a jolly good fellow—
And you needn't be back 'sharp at eight.'

and more briefly:

Far from the maddening crowd
Two miles from the nearest pub
But with Mrs Tame it's 'hame from hame'
And she gives you wonderful grub.

Mrs Tame has had many parsons to stay with her, and once an archbishop spent his honeymoon at her cottage. One of her clergyman visitors wrote the following poem of which this is merely an extract:

. . . Mrs Caiger cried 'Ahoy!
It's time we moved again, my boy!'
Last year it rained and poured and dribbled
I simply sat at home and scribbled.
Lets hope this time wont come as wet
For we're off to Somerset,
To comfy rooms and lovely scenery
Rolling moors and woodland greenery

Mrs Tame just knows the way
To make a perfect holiday
Get the car and grease it well
Tune it up to go like—
And here's a ton of sweets, we'll suck 'em
As we go rolling back to Luccombe.

July '32

EXMOOR VILLAGE, W.J. TURNER (1947)

Not surprisingly there was reluctance to discuss the charges or 'terms' for accommodation although it would have been interesting to know what the much lauded Mrs Tame charged her appreciative guests. Has the standard of guest-houses declined, or are such literary eulogies beyond the capabilities of most of today's guests?

For an imaginative view of Dunster we turn to Mr Presland, who managed to tear himself away from the charms of Lynton and Lynmouth long enough to visit:

To anyone who loves England, and beauty which is so characteristically English, where the love of the present day is visibly linked with the love of the past through long centuries of security, where age has ripened all, the great old trees, the colours of old oak and weatherbeaten tiles and warm brick has gently undulated straight lines and softened all sharp angles, where the very sunlight has the mellowness of old wine, to a mind perceptive of this peculiar and intimate charm of England, Dunster makes a special call, set amid the suave curves of its rich country, crowned by its ancient castle, dignified by its old beautiful church (grown, like the castle, through Norman and Early English and Perpendicular styles of architecture) yet intimate and familiar, and beautiful most of all because of the use and wont of daily life within its walls.

LYNTON AND LYNMOUTH, J. PRESLAND (1918)

Major historical events have, in the main, left Exmoor untouched. Remote from the political centres, and well away from the seat of power, uprisings,

DUNSTER

plots and intrigues, and even the Civil War, were unimportant events that passed by. Dunster Castle suffered, staunchly Royalist, and as a result of its involvement on the wrong side was formally defortified, but the armies came no further westward in this direction, as described by C. Chadwyck Healey:

So far as we can see these westernmost parishes were but little influenced by great popular disturbances. The revolting Cornishmen in 1497 passed the district to the eastward at Taunton, and in 1549 the strife between the King's party and the Cornish and Devon rebels under Sir Humphrey Arundell and the Mayor of Bodmin, although near, does not seem to have affected the peace of the district. Possibly some stir was made when the commissioners appointed by Henry VIII, in 1539 for the defence of the coasts of Somerset and Devon prepared their plans. Amongst the Cottonian MSS, in the British Museum there is a plan . . . showing 'the coste of England uppon Seuerne.' We see two block-houses, each with two guns, near Porlock, one between the town and sea, the other at Hurlstone Point. I cannot find that they were ever erected. Many such forts or block-houses were built or furnished during that year, of which we have particulars, but the Severn defences do not appear to be mentioned. Probably the plan was part of the scheme of the commissioners, but was never carried into effect.

The great Civil War came nearer home. Luccombe and Selworthy were not long in attracting the attention of the Parliament. An attempt was made to arrest Dr. Bryan in his refectory house at the former place, and both parishes were for a time garrisoned by soldiers of the Parliament, to the great tribulation of Mr. Steynings at Holnicote. The dragoons, 'at least forty will not only have hay but oats too for their horses, so that we shall hardly "eat hay with our horse," as the old saying is, ere winter overpass.' The sieges of Dunster Castle, too, must have affected our district. Mr. Wingfield, at Blackford, excused his delay in completing his submission to the Parliament, by his fear of reprisals by the King's people then at Dunster.

Monmouth's rebellion, there is good reason to believe, was not without recruits from Luccombe and Porlock. The parish officers of Luccombe journeyed to Bridgwater and Stogumber 'about the rebells and their estates.' Two rebels were hanged at Porlock, three at Dunster and six at Minehead.

The Black Death did not leave Exmoor untouched, and the effects were felt throughout the whole country:

There is unfortunately little to show to what extent the ravages of the Black Death were felt in our district. That the terrible pestilence was at work within it we cannot doubt. First heard of in the Crimea, it spread all over the Mediterranean shores, crossed France, and in August, 1348, landed at Melcombe Regis in Dorset. It affected the whole of the kingdom, and passed on to Scotland and Ireland. In England alone from one third to one half, according to various estimates, of the entire population perished. Its consequences were far-reaching, the whole face of rural England was changed. Her agricultural system was transformed, and a new direction was given to her industries. It affected the whole future course of her political, social, and economic life.

The Black Death reached the county of Somerset about the early autumn at the latest, of 1348, and it was at its height in December in that year and in January and February, 1349, and appears to have remained for some months after. Father Gasquet has relied principally upon the institutions by the Bishops in proof of the great mortality amongst the clergy, and thereby, inferentially, showing the suffering of the laity. The number of institutions by the Bishop of Bath and Wells during the ciritical period are given in the following little table:

1348		1349					
Nov	Dec	Jan	Feb	Mar	April	May	June
9	32	47	43	36	40	21	7

MINEHEAD

The reader may see from my lists of the rectors in this district that there was an institution at Stoke Pero in December, 1348, and another in February following. At Culbone there was also an institution in February. The following April saw a vacancy at Porlock. We are not expressly told that these vacancies were caused by death, but we can hardly doubt it. There was an institution at Stoke Pero between the two to which I have referred above, but that is in so many words said to have been caused by resignation. The methodical silence of the record as to the cause of the vacancies during those fatal months when bands of priests journeyed almost daily to the Bishop at Wiveliscombe to be instituted is grimly expressive. There was another institution at Culbone in January, 1349–50, which looks rather late for a death by the pestilence, but it is quite possible that the vacancy was so caused, for the scourge lingered later in Devon. If we look for what happened in neighbouring parishes we find that at Winsford there was an institution in February, 1348–9, one at Dulverton in the same month and one at Minehead in March following. Cutcombe suffered severely. There was a vacancy in December, 1348. The 'poor clerk' who filled it, so described in the record of his institution. Not a few 'poor clerks' and chaplains were appointed to livings then. This, be it remembered, is but a record of the losses amongst the incumbents, but the *capellani*, the unbeneficed clergy of the district, without doubt suffered as much, if not more. I cannot trace the death of a local lord from this cause, but it is not improbable that Sir Robert de Stockhey of Porlock was a victim.

HISTORY OF PARTS OF WEST SOMERSET, C. CHADWYCK HEALEY (1901)

Although Minehead lies just outside the boundaries of Exmoor National Park it does belong to the moor, for its history and its people are closely linked. Had it not already been 'developed' it would surely have come within the confines. As it is, Minehead is the principal town of the north-eastern area of Exmoor, and the inhabitants look upon it as their playground – and their livelihood.

A scathing indictment to the ruthless exploitation of old Minehead comes from the pen of J.L.W. Page. He describes the bleak development that all too often accompanied the 'opening up' of the coastal resorts. Sad to relate, little has changed today, and those in power have failed to learn the lessons of history:

The town gathers unto itself stark regiments of brick and mortar called 'streets,' and detached boxes of like material, called 'villas'; perhaps a tall, unsightly factory chimney overshadows the landscape, or a brick-field poisons the air with odours stifling as those of the bottomless pit. At all events, dark lines of metal rule the face of the land with unerring precision, bearing the noisy train and still noisier excursionist to the once peaceful and still beautiful country. Everyone who reads these pages can probably call to mind one or more rural districts 'spoilt' by that civilization whose ruthless pioneer is a locomotive, and whose sapper and miner that much-to-be-abused gentleman, the speculative builder. That Minehead still retains most of its former charm is certainly due neither to the first or second factor, but rather to the good taste of the ground-landlord and his agents.

Yet the place has changed. Where is the old overhung 'Watery Lane' that erewhile passed from the tanyard to the sea? Where the paved pathway that led from the Quay Town to the church? where the shady repose of the New Road? Alas! the first lies buried beneath the Avenue, a wide highway bordered by modern villas; the second, although still existing in part, has had its upper end destroyed to make way for new roads and newer buildings; while the last, though still 'shady,' can scarcely be called reposeful, when every summer day a cheap train deposits at the station, on the very verge of the beach, its consignment of pleasure-seekers. But if certain elements of the picturesque and peaceful have been swept away, let us be thankful that most still remains untouched, and be grateful to those who have offered up at the shrine of modern enterprise so few of the older, and perhaps, for that very reason, the more attractive objects at Minehead.

EXMOOR, J.L.W. PAGE (1890)

EIGHT

Towards the South

Travel by rail was the norm in the early days of the twentieth century and the railway companies did their utmost to extol the virtues of the countryside served by their routes. In 1928 the Great Western Railway published a fat book on GLORIOUS DEVON. The author, S.P.B. Mais, was a friend and frequent guest of Henry Williamson, and his literary skills and perception lift this work way above more routine guides. He begins his chapter on Exmoor thus:

Nothing could well be more different from Dartmoor than Exmoor, but the way to get to know them is identically the same. It is just to encircle them like a child eating round the edge of a plate of hot rice pudding, and then to cut right through the heart of them by way of their rivers.

Having now nibbled round the edges we are at liberty to explore the heart of Exmoor. Both the main Exmoor rivers pass close to Dulverton, and perhaps the best of all circular tours is to be got by tracing the Barle to its source and then coming home down the Exe. The wooded stretches of the brown Barle, past lovely Hawkridge are known to all fishermen, for it is even more famous than the Otter, but archaeologists also follow its winding banks to see Tarr Steps, a cyclopean bridge of unknown origin composed of twenty blocks raised three feet out of the water supporting massive flat granite slabs. But while the antiquarian wistfully searches for theories as to their history, the lover of beauty is content to stand on them and just let his eyes dwell on the exquisite combination of moorland, rich valley, woodland, and waterway. After a few more bends in the river we reach the tiny village of Withypool, which is as delightful as its name, and after that the trees become more sparse and the country opens out until we reach Simonsbath, the capital of the moor, a village of larches and firs, an admirable centre not only for anglers but for all walkers. It is from here that one realises how ridiculous it is to compare Dartmoor with Exmoor.

Simonsbath has infinite riches set in a little room. The cream of Exmoor can all be explored, and with very little difficulty, from its doors. Though you may encounter wild storms you will never run the same danger of getting lost that you do on Dartmoor. Dartmoor has no village in its very centre. It is too inhuman for that. Exmoor, whose spirit is more kindly, welcomes one. There are four roads running out of Simonsbath, and each one leads to a fresh fairyland. Our way lies straight on along the stony lane to Challacombe, below which runs the Barle, getting perceptibly narrower until at Goat Hill, where it passes underneath the road, it is a mere brook babbling over loose boulders on a treeless moor. We leave the road to follow it, and within a mile are at Pinkery Pond on Hoar Oak Hill, having triumphantly and very easily tracked it to its source.

Exe Head lies due east over untracked boggy moorland the loneliness of which is accentuated by its one stunted oak tree. The great river actually rises one mile to the south of the tree, and then makes its way east under the road about a mile south of Brendon Two Gates, which is the county boundary, and meanders down a desolate ravine parallel with Haccombe Water to Exford. This is by far the best angle from which first to explore the Doone Valley, for the descent to it from Exe Head really is rough and not too easy to find, and you have the additional advantage of coming on the famous valley from the moor itself, instead of from the civilised and much-trodden way of Badgworthy. As Blackmore lived on this side it is obvious that this must have been the approach best known to him.

EXFORD FROM THE BRIDGE

As you flounder about on these bog-ridden heights, and see deer no higher than the giant bracken peering out at you, some of the legends that you heard in childhood seem less improbable than they did in the security of Oare and Malmsmead, Exford, or Simonsbath. It is not so easy to be pixy-led as it is at Cranmere, but it wouldn't do to deny the pixies' power or their existence on Lanacombe or Swap Hill.

Re-read Whyte-Melville's 'Katerfelto,' re-read 'Lorna Doone,' and Fortescue's 'Story of a Red Deer,' and you will find three different entrancing angles from which to approach this really unknown tract of lovely country. Then come to it in person, and fish its waters from seven-bridged Winsford to Exford, from Dulverton to Simonsbath, ride to hounds or run to them on foot over moor and vale, and let Exmoor have her way with you. You will soon cease to worry about her minuteness. You will find enough variety, wealth of scenery, and occupation to make a holiday spent on it in every way memorable.

Having exhausted the charms of the Barle and the Exe and the moors above them, there remains on the southern side the country of Dane's Brook and Lytton Water, of Molland Moor and North Molton ridge, and the enchanting reaches of the River Mole, on whose banks lies the home of Tom Faggus, the highwayman, and a church and old mansion that even in Devon stand out as remarkable. Finally climb out of Simonsbath by the south-western road past the iron mine at Blue Gate above the Barle ravine, and stand at Kinsford Gate looking down through Yard Gate on to the rich blue weald of mid-Devon and the black tors of distant Dartmoor, and you will agree that scenery in other lands may rise perhaps to greater heights, but nothing more definitely satisfying to the aesthetic mind is likely to be found in an imperfect world.

Entering a little town (Dulverton) the road is jammed tight between cottages; so narrow is the lane that foot passengers huddle up in doorways to avoid the touch of the wheels, and the windows of the houses are protected by iron bars like cages lest the splashboards should crack the glass. Nowhere in closest-built London is there such a lane—one would imagine land to be dear indeed. The farm labourers, filing homewards after their day's work, each carry poles of oak or faggots on their shoulders for their hearths, generally oak branches; it is their perquisite. The oak somehow takes root among the interstices of the stones of this rocky land. Past the houses the rush! rush! of the brown barley rises again in the still evening air.

'SUMMER IN SOMERSET', RICHARD JEFFERIES (1887)

Long vanished from the scene is the monastic influence. Barlynch Priory is now a farm, a few crumbling stones and a name on the map. Yet in the thirteenth century the Prior of Taunton was given the whole town, manor and hundred of Dulverton, and their presence is recalled by the Revd William Gresswell:

There is something romantic about these monastic holdings in the wild districts of Exmoor, so far as they convey to us a portion of the medieval spirit and give us a glimpse of those shadowy days when

WINSFORD

Depulsare, simpulsare, compulsare, all meant a different method of striking with a hammer or clapper, rather than swinging the bells. The story goes that when the great bell of Barlynch was taken down to Exeter Cathedral from the valley of the Exe it refused to sound a note. 'What new place is this?' the 'Big Ben' might have said. 'Why should I who have for generations struck the note of Primes and Terces, Sexts and Nones at Barlynch be asked to call strangers together in a strange city for a strange service?' Perhaps the indignity of swinging the big bell might have been tried! At all events, when it did send out a sonorous note—so rumour says—it turned all the Devonshire cream sour in that Devonshire capital! . . .

The priors of Taunton had hunting traditions even in Saxon times, since the days of Edward the Elder, if not before, when they gave the king's hunting and hawking parties 'pastum unius noctis,' together with assistance on the road westwards from Taunton towards Williton, Exmoor and the west. When the Prior of Taunton became the squire and parson, practically, of the whole of Dulverton, it is not likely that he allowed the hunting and sporting traditions of his house to die out. Although he may have abjured hunting himself, still many of his retinue and minor dependents did not do so but were always expected to keep the larder of the central establishment going. Many of the outlying monastic holdings such as Adscombe, belonging to Athelney on the Quantocks, and Bossington, belonging to the same abbey and at one time within Exmoor Forest, were said to be 'in victu monachorum,' and no doubt supplied fish and venison and game generally.

From another point of view—that of the archaeologist—it may be deplored that in the church of Dulverton, linked so closely to Taunton of old, there are so few signs of a monastic règime which, although it was condemned clearly enough in its general working, nevertheless filled such a long and picturesque place in the local annals. Now it is a chapter over which there is almost the stillness of the grave. Who knows or cares much where the priory of Taunton stood?

FORESTS AND DEER PARKS OF THE COUNTY OF SOMERSET,

REVD WM GRESSWELL (1905)

old abbeys and priories, great and small, greeted the eye sometimes in the most unlooked for corners. Who, travelling over the rough and wild expanses of Exmoor, would have dreamed of lighting, for example, upon Barlynch Priory nestling by the Exe? What a contrast to the bleak uplands and heathery slopes of Winsford Hill is this cosy nook of the Black Canons of Brompton Regis! Here arose what is sometimes grandiloquently called an abbey! A ruined wall or so is all that remains of what must have been, after all, a fair array of monastic buildings: the barns, granary, sheds, linhays, and, above all, a monastic church. Tradition says that here was a bell-tower with several bells, which, at the time of the Dissolution, in King Henry the VIII's reign, were scattered abroad. How sweet and solemn at times must these Barlynch bells have sounded up that echoing glen, mingling their tones with the everlasting rippling melody of the Exe. It was a chime, probably, rather than a peal that the monks sounded for their services from prime to compline, for ringing with bell-ropes and a swinging cradle was not always the fashion in mediaeval times.

BARLINCH PRIORY

An early view of Simonsbath

From Dulverton it is a short distance to that famous tourist attraction – Tarr Steps. Jefferies followed the river to partake of that West Country delicacy now known as a cream tea.

The brown Barle enjoys his life, and splashes in the sunshine like boys bathing—like them he is sunburnt and brown. He throws the wanton spray over the ferns that bow and bend as the cool breeze his current brings sways them in the shade. He laughs and talks, and sings louder than the wind in his woods. . . .

Following the current downwards at last the river for a while flows in quietness, broad and smooth. A trout leaps for a fly with his tail curved in the air, full a foot out of water. Trout watch behind sunken stones, and shoot to and fro as insects droop in their flight and appear about to fall. So clear is the water and so brightly illuminated that the fish are not easily seen—for vision depends on contrast—but in a minute I find a way to discover them by their shadows. The black shadow of a trout is distinct upon the bottom of the river, and guides the eye to the spot, then looking higher in the transparent water there is the fish. It was curious to see these black shadows darting to and fro as if themselves animated and without bodies, for if the trout darted before being observed the light concealed him in motion. Some of the trout came up from under Torre-steps, a singular structure which here connects the shores of the stream. Everyone has seen a row of stepping stones across a shallow brook; now pile other stones on each of these, forming buttresses, and you have the plan of the primitive bridge. It has a megalithic appearance, as if associated with the age of rude stone monuments. They say its origins are doubtful; there can be no doubt of the loveliness of the spot. The Barle comes with his natural rush and fierceness under the unhewn stone planking, then deepens, and there overhanging a black pool—for the shadow was so deep as to be black—grew a large bunch of marsh marigolds in fullest flower, the broad golden cups almost resting on the black water. The bridge is not intended for wheels, and though it is as firm as the rock, foot passengers have to look at their steps, as the great planks, flecked with lichen at the edges, are not all

level. The horned sheep and lambs go over it—where do they not go? Like goats they wander everywhere.

In a cottage some way up the hill we ate clotted cream and whortleberry jam. Through the open door came the ceaseless rush! rush! like a wind in the wood. The floor was of concrete, lime and sand, on the open hearth,—pronounced 'airth'—sods of turf cut from the moor, and oak branches were smouldering under the chimney crook. Turf smoke from the piled-up fires of winter had darkened the beams of the ceiling, but from that rude room there was a view of the river, and the hill, and the oaks in full June colour, which the rich would envy.

'SUMMER IN SOMERSET', RICHARD JEFFERIES (1887)

Elihu Burritt, the energetic American who walked from London to Land's End and back, found Dulverton a romantic spot. He had walked from Molland along the crest of the moor which he found an exhilarating experience:

On one side was the cold, rocky region covered with furze, ferns and heather, on the other a fertile, smiling world of beauty all bright, warm and glad with the glow of life and cultivated nature.

Toward sunset, I descended from the rough, stony foot-paths of the moor to the turnpike road, which wound its way down among the high, heavily-wooded hills to the village of Dulverton, in Somerset, as romantic a place as I ever saw. The winding glen was narrow and deep, walled in by lofty heights and mostly covered with trees. But here and there, new-shorn meadows, soft and smooth as lawns, flashed out of the thick shade like patches of green sunlight. Through the pent valley bending around the bases of these towering heights, there rippled, dashed, flashed and ran a little river, gurgling and giggling under moss and ivy-netted bridges and arches of over-branching trees. Here and there a mill, quaint and olden, straddled the swift-footed stream, and dipped its dripping wheel into it. There were cottages that would sit well to an artist—some fronting hard upon the narrow road, some hung up, or shelved in niches cut in the sides of the steep and lofty hills. Some were so completely webbed and covered with ivy to the chimney-top, that only an eye or two looked out through an aperture in the thick mass of foliage. All the natural elements were present to make it an interesting *locale* for a romance, if any human experience were found in the village to match the uniqueness of the scenery. Indeed, a novelist stopping in Dulverton a week, would hardly fail to lay down the airy beams of a fiction founded on fact. It is the very focus of radiation for a tourist bent on recreation and invigorating exercise and bold adventure.

Mr Burritt was obviously a farmer back in the USA, and was sufficiently interested in native breeds of cattle to deviate from his route to visit Mr Quartley at Molland. How sad they would both be at the virtual demise of such breeds, to be replaced by the ubiquitous Friesians:

On reaching South Moulton, I found that Mr. Quartley, the celebrated breeder of Devonsire cattle, resided full seven miles beyond, at a place called Molland. So, the next morning, I went on to his establishment, planted on a lofty hill, and overlooking some of the most picturesque valleys in Devonshire. Leaving the main road, I ascended to it by a winding path among the trees, which, if they broke the scorching force of a July sun, also seemed to bate the breath of the breeze, so that no air circulated under their thick branches. It was the hottest day I had seen on my journey, and I was glad to reach the summit, and find, after all, there was a little refreshing air breathing still at that height. Mr. Quartley was at dinner, and invited me to a seat at the table with that easy and genial hospitality which one associates with the good old-fashioned farmers of this country. The house was just like his hospitality, a kind of old English mansion or manor-house, being divided by a broad hall, with one door opening upon the road, the other upon a green lawn, well belted with shrubbery. After dinner, he took me over his fields and showed me a herd of cows, all of the purest Devon blood. He winters from seventy to eighty head, including about twenty milking cows. He sells calves from six to eight months old at from thirty to seventy guineas, averaging £40 each. The cows produce on an average five pounds of

butter a week in the pasture season. They were truly beautiful animals, and I was glad to see how the breed we so much prize in America looked at home, in the purest form and aspect of the blood. It was well worth a long and special journey to see them. Take them all in all, putting form against form, and feature against feature, I think no hoofed and horned animal equals the pure Devonshire for delicate symmetry of shape and structure, and for a variety of graces which you can find in no other blood. Everything is perfect in them, and all things in happy proportion. In a Devonshire heifer you do not see a highly-bred lady in a coarse salt-and-pepper suit, with a pair of rough, short, twisted hair-pins curling at unlevel curves inward upon her forehead, as is often the case with the Shorthorn. There is a delicacy about her form that beautifies animal life, and means something more than beef. Her deep-red robe of silky softness fits her body and limbs without pucker or wrinkle, and shows the grace of their make and movement as under a veil of gossamer. Then her eyes, so honest, round and pure under their lashes with the light of good dispositions—so full of tender and intelligent expression that one, looking into them as a man with a heart in him should look, is inclined to believe that this very blood existed in the mythological ages, and these very eyes were the ones the ancients had in their minds and put between the lids of Juno, as the most distinguishing grace and measure of her beauty. Then there are her incomparable horns, fitting and befitting her head like a diadem. None ever worn by any other bovine race, of higher pretensions, are so perfect and beautiful. They crown and embody all her other symmetries. They measure and seemingly regulate their development. They outgrow no proportion, nor fall short of any; but are to each in parity what the pupil is to the human eye. Their downward, outward and winding curves show a grace, from root to tip, which could never be given them by human hand or art on a forming block. Then their peculiar transparency illumines this grace of form, adding a feature that completes their beauty as a pearly crowning for the head and protecting shield and ornament for the face. For more than half a century the Devonshire oxen, or cattle *graded* with the blood, have

BURY BRIDGE

stood the test of our stony New England hills. Their patient, intelligent, enduring toil at the plough, cart and sled has been more intimately associated with farm-labor with us in all seasons than that of any other race. For all these years they have bent their breasts to the bow and dragged the hot ploughshare over hill and valley, often with the mercury at ninety degrees in the shade. They have sunk in the mire of our swamps to the hips and there lay, without fractious floundering, with quiet and hopeful eyes fixed upon their master, until they were unyoked, and could rise to a footing on the surface, one by one. They have wallowed through the deep and drifting snows, making paths for men and more impatient animals, and hauling down loads of oak, walnut and maple from the mountains for the fuel of our winter fires. What New England man at home or abroad, who ever drank in the air of his country's hills or shared or saw its industrial life, can dissociate from its pleasant memories the Old Red Oxen of Massachussetts and Connecticut! Not I. The whole vista of my boyhood is full of their forms and remembrances; and here, on this Devonshire hill, with the purest specimens of the race before me, I would offer a small tribute to their memory and their worth.

A WALK FROM LONDON TO LAND'S END AND BACK, ELIHU BURRITT (1834)

From Molland it is but a short distance to South Molton, the capital of southern Exmoor:

Among the parishes enumerated, Southmolton holds the principal place. The town takes its name from the river Moul, or Mole, which riseth about five miles distant to the north-ward, on the forest of Exmoor, and runs thro' the parish from north to south, and at a few miles distance falls into the river Taw. Its length, from east to west, exceeds half a mile, and from north to south it is nearly the same. It consists of two large wide streets, besides two others of a smaller extent.

About the year 1780, the inhabitants of the town and parish did not exceed 2500. In the late return under the population act, they were *2753*. The situation is esteemed healthy. The ruins and poor remains of some gentlemen's seats are still subsisting; but as they have been alienated, and sold to different people, who do not reside upon them, they are dwindled into farm-houses, and of course not worthy of notice.

At the eastern end is a stone bridge of arches, which parts the parish from Bishop's Nymett. About two miles distance from the town, on the south, is another stone bridge of arches, which parts it from Mariansleigh; another in the same manner between this parish and Chittlehamton; a fourth not far distant between this town and Filleigh. These bridges are repaired partly by particular estates, and partly by the adjoining parishes. Some good and valuable woods lie within its limits, consisting of the usual produce of this part of the country. Roads not to be highly extolled – the best are turnpike; but even these in some measure indifferent. Within this parish are several good farm-houses, and valuable estates belonging to them: Only two villages, both on the western side; their names Hill and Shallow ford.

HISTORY OF DEVONSHIRE, REVD RICHARD POLWHELE (1806)

NINE

The Heart of the Forest

I regret to have to record that Exmoor, as a forest, is a delusion and a fraud. Even in 1651, when the last perambulation of it was ordered, there was only one tree, known as the Kite Oak. This tree stood on the hill marked today as Kittuck, and one tree will never make a forest.

EXMOOR: THE RIDING PLAYGROUND OF ENGLAND, CECIL ALDIN (1935)

The boundaries of the forest have varied considerably over the centuries, and were at their most extensive in King John's day when the Royal Chase covered some 80,000 acres including Porlock, Dulverton, Withypool and Culbone, although the king appears never to have taken advantage of his royal prerogative.

The bounds were decided by 'perambulations' of which there have been several. Records survive of those in 1279, 1298 and a Parliamentary Survey of 1651. This last reduced the size of the forest to more or less its present bounds:

Taking the 1279 Perambulation as our guide, it is perfectly clear that the manor of Dulverton and the woods of Nicholas de Bonvile lay outside the forest and they formed part of the property of Thomas de Pyne before N. de Bonvile married his widow and so inherited them. In Domesday the 'wood' of Dulverton is described as one mile long and half-a-mile broad, and it belonged to Count Harold. Or could it be that Dulverton wood, originally Crown demesne, was always regarded as a 'Dominicus boscus' in spite of any act of disafforestation? This appears to be only alternative unless we suppose that the Act of 1279 fell still-born. The history of these Dominici bosci or Crown preserves, outside the perambulations, is

not always clear. When the Prior of Taunton was given the whole town, manor and hundred of Dulverton, did he hold Dulverton wood absolutely and by the same tenure as he held the rest?

Another interesting question is the date at which the forest of Exmoor was first perambulated. In Saxon times it was probably a huge indeterminate area of forest land. But in Norman times it was, together with Dartmoor, first placed 'in Regard' in the reign of Henry I. May we not conclude that then was the date of the earliest perambulation?

In the first instance the old forest appears to have been located entirely within the county of Somerset, as the western boundary is always given as the forest and county boundary. But in Stuart times certain Devon manors appear to have been included, their owners appearing as 'Lords of the Chase.'

FORESTS AND DEER PARKS OF THE COUNTY OF SOMERSET,
REVD WM GRESSWELL (1905)

The final perambulation took place in 1815, subsequent to what was planned as a huge act of enclosure, and resulted in the formation of the new parish of Exmoor.

Reading early descriptions of the heartland of the moor it is perhaps not so surprising that it was generally avoided. The bleak heights to which the forest was ultimately reduced were not favoured by the deer any more than they were by the local farmers, though it would appear that a hardier race of men once lived, or at any rate died, on the moor.

The bailiwick of this forest was usually held by people of distinction. In the time of Hen. III, it was held by William de Placetis, by

CAMP AT EXEBRIDGE, 16 SEPTEMBER 1929

the service of paying to the King four heifers, and a young bull, or for each of them ten pence.

The office of forester continued for many years afterwards in the family of Peche, and is now held of the crown by Sir Thomas Acland, bart.

As the only produce of this wild tract is pasturage, it is principally stocked with sheep, and a small breed of horses and cattle from the adjoining parishes. There are a few wild deer; but these are more numerous on the adjacent commons, and the neighbouring woods contain a great many of this sort of animal. Many curious plants and flowers flourish here, and in the neighbouring country; particularly the erica and the hawkweed; the digitalis, blue scabius, and yellow tormentilla, intermixed with some scarce lichens and polypodies, which with their blended tints enliven the scene, and delight the traveller.

But here, upon this desolate spot, which perhaps never experienced the labours of the industrious husbandman, but has remained the same for a long succession of many thousand years; the eye of reflection sees stand uninterrupted a number of simple sepulchres of departed souls, whether of warriors, priests, or kings, it matters not; their names have long been buried with their persons in the dust of oblivion; and their memories have perished with their mouldering urns. A morsel of earth now damps in silence the *eclat* of noisy warriors; and the green turf serves as a sufficient shroud for kings!

In this neighbourhood also are many of those circular intrenchments, which in our maps are called castles; but from the inconsiderable size of some, and the situation of others, a doubt may be admitted whether they were ever intended for military purposes. They are assuredly vestiges of antiquity; and perhaps they might have been thrown up in the early ages of Druidism, for the celebration of religious rites and ceremonies; or in later days, for seats of activity or athletick exhibitions. Cow-Castle, indeed, situated on the river Barle, northwest from Withypool, is an exception to the foregoing observations.

This is the farthest extremity of the county westward towards Devonshire. There is a farm in the forest called *Symonsbath*, remote from any other habitation, where runs a small river rising northwest, which hereabout joins the Ex, and has over it a wooden bridge. The western extremity of this forest is a point at right angles, called *Sadler's Stone*, near the head of the rivers Ex and Barle.

HISTORY AND ANTIQUITIES OF THE COUNTY OF SOMERSET, REVD JOHN COLLINSON (1791)

'A useless and void space in the map of the County of Somerset' is how the Forest of Exmoor was described in 1795, showing it had changed little in over one hundred years since the early travellers equally condemned its barren and inhospitable nature.

But John Billingsley saw further. The purpose of his visit was to study the possibility of agricultural improvement for the Board of Agriculture, set up in 1793 as a result of the interruption of foreign food supplies because of the frequent wars. His book had the grand title of GENERAL VIEW OF THE AGRICULTURE OF THE COUNTY OF SOMERSET, WITH OBSERVATION ON THE MEANS OF ITS IMPROVEMENTS.

John Billingsley's recommendations, made twenty-five years prior to the sale of the Crown lands, make interesting reading. They are certainly (in many instances) prophetic:

In an Agricultural Survey of the county of Somerset, it will naturally be expected that particular notice should be taken of the forest of Exmoor; its vast extent, and capability of improvement, render it an object well worthy of attention.

This forest extends from North to South about eight miles, and from East to West ten or twelve; containing, according to an accurate survey lately made, about nineteen thousand nine hundred acres. Nearly at the centre of this large tract of land is an estate called *Simonsbath*, inclosed, and consisting of about two hundred acres, with a dwelling-house, licensed and frequented as an inn; and all offices belonging to it convenient for the management of the farm, and transacting the concerns of the forest. Here the forester has an annual sale for the small horses that are bred on the surrounding hills; and here also, during the month of May, he meets the farmers from all the country round, who enter in his books the number of sheep which are depastured with him, at the rate of five-pence per head. The small horses (in the whole upwards of four hundred) are not taken into better keeping, nor to more sheltered grounds, during the severest winter. When the snow covers the forest to the depth of many feet, these hardy animals are seen in droves, traversing the little vallies and sheltered parts, gathering their scanty fare from the banks of rivulets and warm springs; but the sheep are almost all driven off for the winter, in the months of November, December, and January, according as the season is more or less severe.

The river Barl runs adjoining to this estate, but resigns its name on being joined by a small stream, about two miles to the East, called the Ex. . . .

On the summits of the hills, and especially on the West and North, are swamps of many acres extent. They are cut up as turf, at the rate of eight-pence or twelve-pence per thousand, paid to the tenant of the forest, and would be an inexhaustible stock of fuel to any inhabitants settling on the better part, as well as of black peat for burning lime, working iron, smelting ore, or any manufacture where fire is used.

The roads are in general, as might be expected in so large a tract of land without inhabitants, very bad, and in some places scarcely passable. But the whole abounds with materials to make them firm and comfortable, at an easy rate, and few bridges would be necessary.

Excepting a few willows and thorns by the sides of the rivulets, not a tree or a bush, out of Simonsbath estate, is to be seen on the whole forest; but plantations of most kinds need no more shelter, nor better soil, than is to be met with here. Oak, firs, beech, and elm, would thrive in all the parts capable of tillage. And a very large proportion of the whole needs but the spirit, and the fortune, of some one or more of our wealthy gentlemen in England, whose attention, if turned this way, sanctioned by the royal proprietor, would render the forest of Exmoor, in a few years, as fair a prospect as the surrounding country; and not an useless and void space, as it now is, in the map of the county of Somerset. The term useless, however, may be said by some to be misapplied, when the quantity of sheep is

mentioned that is depastured on it. From the best information to be had, twenty-two thousand are summered here, besides the four hundred horses beformentioned; but the race is so small, and their value so trifling, that little profit accrues to the owner. Veins both of copper and iron have been discovered, that might be worked to advantage, considering how convenient the situation is for shipping off the produce; Porlock, Lynmouth, and Combmarten, all sea-ports, not being more than nine miles distant from the centre of the forest.

From each of those places, and also from Ilfracombe and Barnstable, vessels are every week passing to Wales (where founderies have been long established) in *ballast*. A large vein of lime-stone is known to pass from East to West near the centre of the forest, and proper stone is found for building on almost every part. And to compleat the whole, *slate* of a good quality has been dug up in large quantities not far from Simonsbath; and there is every reason to think it may be found in other places. Water is in plenty in every part, as beforementioned: and several market-towns are within a few miles of the forest. Large tracts of land are well adapted for the tillage of flax, which is known to thrive best on old or unvegetated ground, with a strong deep soil.

The grain which thrives in the adjoining parishes would, no doubt, flourish here; and a ready sale would be found in the neighbouring markets, or by being exported from the ports on the Bristol channel.

The ashes, arising from the weeds and other extraneous matter on the surface being burnt, mixed with lime, would be a first dressing, preparatory to a crop of turnips or corn.

From the produce of the crops would arise manure for future tillage; and what is now a barren waste, might be made worth from five to twenty shillings per acre.

The plan for inclosures and buildings on the forest, I would recommend, is this: Let there be a small town or village erected near the middle, suppose by Simonsbath-house, which should form proper residences for artificers and husbandmen, to be employed in building farm-houses, and inclosing many a comfortable estate round them.

The Vicarage, Simonsbath, Devon

THE VICARAGE, SIMONSBATH

From this centre town, or village, it would be easy to get a supply of provisions and all other necessaries, as a butcher, baker, shopkeeper, &c. might be there settled. And, till other houses or villages should be built, labourers, artificers, and workmen, might find lodgings, provisions, &c. in the bordering parishes, many of which, at this time, have more labourers than they can well employ. The method of fencing, cultivating, manuring, &c. would vary but little from the plan adopted on Mendip hills; and if prosecuted with vigour, would tend to lessen the poor's rates, and would train up a rising generation to care and industry, instead of theft and idleness.

GENERAL VIEW OF AGRICULTURE OF THE COUNTY OF SOMERSET, JOHN BILLINGSLEY

(1795)

Billingsley's moral tone strikes a chord; it seems there really is nothing new in this age of ours except the way in which some of us look at the countryside. Billingsley saw only a barren landscape capable of becoming reasonable farm land supporting a community. Today we would fight hard for the preservation of such scenery—fast vanishing wild moorland, still quite common in 1795 but rare today.

Until the nineteenth century the only dwelling at Simonsbath was Simonsbath House, or Lodge, built in 1654 for James Boevey. He was the Warden of the Forest in the days of Charles I and briefly freeholder during the days of the Commonwealth. The Knights planned a new, grander mansion for themselves behind the old house, and work began but was gradually abandoned as other projects assumed more pressing importance. With the death of Sir Frederick Knight's only son in 1879, work was abandoned altogether. The shell was finally demolished in 1899 and today it is hard to find any trace, but MURRAY'S HANDBOOK of 1865 mentions 'the ruinous wall and flanking towers commenced by Mr Knight':

Simonsbath is a solitary settlement in a moorland valley, encircled by some fine old trees, originally planted as shelter to a rough house of entertainment which formerly stood here. The place consists of Mr. Knight's unfinished mansion, now a picturesque ruin, a small house adjoining it, occupied occasionally as a residence by the present lord of Exmoor, a small public-house, and various out-buildings,

CORONATION OF KING GEORGE V CELEBRATIONS, 1911, DUNKERY BEACON

including the shop of a blacksmith, the yard of a carpenter, and the store of a general dealer. . . .

Exmoor occupies an area of about 14 sq. m., and is still to a great extent uncultivated—a waste of dark hills and valleys tracked by lonely streams. It attains its greatest elevation on the E., where *Dunkery Beacon* rises 1668 ft. above the sea; but on the W. its hills are of little inferior height, *Chapman Barrows* being 1540 ft., and *Span Head* 1610 ft. On its borders it is pierced by deep wooded ravines, of which the traveller has a magnificent example in Lyndale. The central part of this region, about 20,000 acres, formed the ancient *Forest of Exmoor*, for which an Act of enclosure was obtained in 1815, when it was purchased by the late John Knight, Esq., of Wolverley Hall, Worcestershire, who proposed converting it to a less interesting but more profitable land of meadows. With this object he encircled the whole forest with a ring fence, and commenced building a castellated mansion at Simonsbath, but this he soon found occasion to abandon, together with many of his projected improvements, for the speculation proved anything but a golden adventure. A considerable acreage has, however, been brought under cultivation, and this is now leased in separate farms by the proprietor of the forest, Mr. Frederick Knight; the principal drawback to success being the strong winds and chilly mists which prevail in so elevated a district. The soil is in general of a fair quality, although the hard sandstones below the soil, being little liable to decompose, are somewhat unfavourable to fertility. Extensive tracts, however, still remain, both in the forest and surrounding highlands, in a state of nature, delighting the eye by the grandeur of their unbroken outline and the rich beauty of their colour; and here, over slopes of heather, interspersed with the dwarf juniper, cranberry, and whortleberry, roams the 'Exmoor pony,' a breed of the native English horse, carefully preserved by Sir Thomas Acland, and the red forest deer, which still makes its lair in the extensive covers on the moor-side. This is the only corner of England in which the red deer is still to be found in a thoroughly wild state. A stag is now and then roused on the Quantock Hills, but Exmoor itself is their head-quarters. . . .

Since the year 1841 the farms on Exmoor have been chiefly under the management of Mr. Robert Smith, the resident agent of Mr Knight, and under his superintendence upwards of 4000 acres have been let on lease, in addition to the land previously occupied. The water-meadows made by this gentleman are well worth the attention of those interested in agriculture.

MURRAY'S HANDBOOK (1865)

A different view was held by Richard Jefferies. He would find it hard to believe his eyes were he to return today to his beloved moor. He believed it was impermeable and unchangeable – that man's puny efforts were doomed before they began. He viewed all attempts at agricultural improvement as a waste of time, and he is one of the few writers who decried the efforts of the Knight family to bring some measure of prosperity to the heartlands of the moor. He wrote in the years when Sir Frederick Knight was struggling, following the death of his son, and shortly before he sold his interests in 1886. Many of the experiments came to nothing; the farms and smallholdings had a hard struggle to survive – but today most present a picture of security, if not prosperity, very different to that painted by Jefferies:

An immense experiment was made some years ago by the owner of a large part of the moors to improve his seventy thousand acres. He caused the surface to be broken up, and lime to be hauled. Walls were built to form enclosures, and when the deer climbed the walls wire was put along, in which wire many deer got hung by their legs, and had to be killed—being injured. A tramway was laid down. Instead of the horned mountain sheep, or 'Porlocks,' Cheviots were introduced. Numerous farmhouses were erected in a substantial manner, and fir copses planted to shelter the inmates and the stock in the yards from the tremendous gales. The land was let to Scotch farmers, who came down from the North to a country almost resembling their own. A mansion like a castle was built in the midst of the wilderness. All these measures were such as would naturally suggest themselves, but only partially succeeded.

The farmhouses are now occupied by Scotch shepherds; if you knock at the door a Scotch face appears, and you are offered a glass of milk, to which you are 'varra' welcome. The boundless heather, the deep glens, and the red deer correspond to the Gaelic accent. The tramway is gone, and the track has disappeared for great part of

EXMOOR FROM THE QUANTOCKS

its length under thick heather. Over the walls the deer climb easily, and the unfinished castle is moss-grown. All that remains is the improvement effected in some places by the mixture of lime and by the efforts of the Northern farmers, some irrigated meadows in the glens, and the farmhouses at long intervals. So far as the general vista – so far as the red deer and the black game – are concerned, Exmoor has not altered one iota. The vast moors have simply swallowed up the efforts of man to conquer them. The details of this experiment explain why Exmoor remains mediaeval. It resists the perpetual nibbling which goes on around the inhabited places. . . .

Why has Exmoor remained in this condition, uncultivated for so many centuries? why does it still defy agriculture and improvement? Three causes present themselves—the nature of the soil, the cost of labour, and the character of the climate. A long winter of eight months, with continuous rains and heavy fogs, is succeeded by a hot, short summer. Though the summer is very hot there are occasional intervals of cold. Sometimes when vapour is sweeping over from the Severn Sea it is accompanied by a wind which chills to the marrow.

RED DEER, RICHARD JEFFERIES (1884)

In the 1890s when Mr J.L.W. Page visited Simonsbath, the dominion of the Knights had been established for almost eighty years and their mark had been left indelibly on their remote moorland kingdom:

A long hill descends into Simonsbath, passing the neat little church and pretty vicarage, to the handful of cottages that make up the metropolis of Exmoor. There is an inn, with the singularly inappropriate name of 'The William Rufus;' an old house – older than it looks – the occasional residence of the lord of Exmoor, Sir Frederick Knight, and the scene of one of the numerous escapades of that notorious outlaw Tom Faggus. Two centuries ago it was an inn, and here Tom put up one night, ignorant of the fact that his foes were on the watch. He was actually captured, but, with that wonderful luck which usually attended him, contrived to make his escape. Behind rise the grim ruins of the mansion commenced by Sir Frederick's father, like so many other Exmoor projects doomed never to see completion. There is a blacksmith's forge, presided over by a communicative Vulcan (who is also postmaster and registrar of births and deaths!), a school, and one or two other habitations, more or less embowered in trees—for Simonsbath is quite a Vallombrosa—and within doors you positively cannot, except in one or two spots, *see* Exmoor at all. The pastures are well drained, and the agent of the late Mr. Knight must be congratulated on the success which has attended his attempts to reclaim Simonsbath from the waste.

EXMOOR, J.L.W. PAGE (1890)

TEN

Of Mines and Things . . .

But the farmer is now likely to be driven by the miner from his settlement on Exmoor. In 1851 a specimen of the white carbonate of iron was sent by Mr. R. Smith to the Great Exhibition. Its value suggested the expediency of a further search, and this led to the discovery of abundant iron-lodes, including the haematites and other ores hitherto supposed peculiar to Staffordshire and S. Wales. Large districts of the moor are now in the hands of three of the principal iron companies in the kingdom, viz. the Ulverstone of Lancashire, and the Dowlais and Plymouth of S. Wales. Their steam machinery is expected to raise about 300,000 tons of iron-ore annually. Two lines for a mineral railway have been surveyed, the one to Porlock, the other to Lynton; but it is not yet determined which will be adopted. A new district ch., erected principally through the exertions of Mr. Knight, was consecrated 1856.

MURRAY'S HANDBOOK (1865)

The Knight's had great expectations of the wealth to be found under the soil, and the moor bears evidence of their endeavours. Fortunately the above vision of a mining kingdom atop the moorland acres never came to fruition, although the tramway referred to by Jefferies was partially built and it is possible to trace its course as it followed the contours on its way from Simonsbath to Porlock. It was never completed.

Mining on the Brendon Hills was more successful and lasted for a period of around fifty years. Watchet Harbour was developed to facilitate the export of the ore to the furnaces of South Wales, and to reach the port a special railway was built. This had one outstanding feature, the Comberow incline, which transcended the height between coastal plane and Brendon Hills, a gradient of

1 in 4 over just ³/₄ of a mile. It opened in 1858 and ran on, even after the mines shut down in 1882, until 1898.

The mining operations must have been quite impressive in their day, and here is an account of that busy period as seen through the eyes of a child. With her father she visited the area in 1865 and was shown round by the manager of the mines, Mr Morgans from Camarthen, who proved to her that railways can go uphill!:

I asked Mr Morgans and he told me the whole story. . . .

In eleven months the line was laid to Roadwater and six months later, at the end of 1857, it was laid to Comberow and work had started on the inclined plane. It was during that year that tragedy occurred when two locomotives collided head on near Washford and Mr. Hopkins' assistant, Mr. James, and two others persons were killed. . . .

At that moment there was a whistle from 'Pontypool,' and I saw the station at Comberow with several trucks waiting in the sidings. With a last pant we stopped at the platform and Mr. Morgans helped me down.

'Now,' he said, 'how would you like to ride up the inclined plane?'

As we emerged from behind the carriage, he pointed upwards, and I gaped with wonder. The railway went up the hillside in an absolutely straight line, cutting through rocks and woods, and it seemed as if it would reach heaven itself. At the top I could just discern a small building, but men, if there were any, were too small to be seen. It is a sight I shall always remember, and I was filled with awe and wonder. When I recovered my breath I said that I thought

PREPARING FOR A RIDE ON THE INCLINE OF THE BRENDON
RAILWAY

railways could not go uphill. Mr. Morgans said I was right (I knew I was), but that the inclined plane with its two sets of rails was a method of overcoming this difficulty.

'You see,' he said, 'there is one truck at the top and one at the bottom, and each is joined to the other by a stout rope which passes round drums at the top. So when the truck at the top descends, it pulls the one at the bottom up.'

'But what about 'Pontypool,' ' I said, 'how does she get up?'

Mr. Morgans gave a deep laugh and said something to father which was quite incomprehensible to me. Father told me later that he was speaking Welsh!

'She stays here,' he said, 'as there is another engine at the top. The carriages stay here, too, because there is no passenger service on the upper section,' he explained.

We were walking towards the foot of the incline when another horse came by, pulling one of the trucks of timber that 'Pontypool' had brought up with us. Leading the horse was a boy, rather younger than I, who kept saying:

'Come on, Dragon, pull up!'

When he reached a white post he stopped. He fastened three chains to the end of the truck and then led the horse away. Mr. Morgans assisted me on to this truck and then, after helping father to mount, climbed on himself. We sat down and Mr. Morgans advised me to face up the slope if I were scared. I was too excited to be scared, so I faced first one way, then another. At that moment a bell rang and an arm on the white post beside us was raised up by means of a wire.

'Here we go,' said Mr. Morgans, 'hold on.'

An iron wire rope running over pulleys right up the incline jerked about and then became taut. Slowly we moved forward and then we began to climb.

'This,' said Mr. Morgans, 'was the most difficult and costly work of the line. You see, it rises one foot in four, and all work had to be done without the aid of horses. Of course, we blasted the rocks with powder, but building embankments at the lower end was so difficult that we had to get a special stationary engine from South Wales to lower the rocks and spoil for them.'

He said that he had managed to open the incline temporarily after one year.

'You see,' he said, 'it had to be opened quickly because the ore was piling up at the mines and there was nowhere to put it. So I decided to blast a way through quickly and lay down temporary rails, although the inclined plane was then of an uneven gradient. And then at night men dug away and relaid the rails before morning. Finally all was complete at the beginning of 1861, after three and a half years of work on the "incline" alone.'

As he talked we were ascending a little faster than walking pace through deep cuttings where ferns were growing in the rock crevices. I could see, on the other side, the descending truck approaching us; it appeared to have no passengers, just a load of iron ore. Then it passed and grew smaller and smaller as it neared the bottom. I could feel the air growing colder the higher we went, and when we finally reached the top after about ten minutes there was a chilly wind blowing. The truck stopped on a high embankment of slaty stone and when I dismounted I looked round. I could see all the way to the sea, and beyond it the coast of Wales, which must be 30 miles away. It was a remarkable view and I was filled with wonder at the majesty of it all . . .

And so it was that at about two o'clock we found ourselves in the changing room of the Raleigh's Cross mine. This is a small stone building containing many hot water pipes for drying men's clothes, and here we put on old clothes to protect us from dirt.

The 'mine compound,' as it is called, is a field by the road, with various large buildings in, some with tall chimneys, and several railway sidings; these join themselves together, cross the road, and pass through another field to the main line at the top of the incline. There is a high hedge round the field and a large pair of white gates forms the only entrance. On one side are some cottages for foremen and the mine office, with a miners' clubroom over; on the other side is a large building with a tall chimney, which, Mr. Morgans said,

contains the massive winding engine for hauling the 'trams' or trucks of ore out of the pit, and a reading-room, provided for the men by the Company. Extending from this winding house to the shaft is a large wooden bridge on which the trams run, so that the ore may be tipped straight into railway wagons on the siding below. Beside the shaft itself is the pump house and, after changing, Mr. Morgans led us thither. It is a tall, stone building and from one end of it, near the top, projects a balcony. Beside this balcony the beam pivots slowly up and down, lifting the large timber pump rods. We entered the building up a flight of stone steps and through an arched door; once inside we were confronted by the huge bulk of the cylinder.

All about was the sound of escaping steam, clanking rods and the resonant thump of the beam, pausing momentarily at the end of its stroke. Mr. Morgans shouted something above the noise and a short man with a pleasant smile emerged from behind the cylinder, wiping his hands on a rag. He doffed his cap and was introduced to us as Mr. Blackwell, the chief engine fitter. He conducted us round the pump house, of which the ground floor was almost filled by the 50-inch cylinder, ten feet high, with the valve gear and steam pipes in front, and the control rods for maintaining the correct strokes. We went up a flight of stairs on to the first floor, through which the top of the cylinder projected, and Mr. Blackwell showed us the piston rod, six inches thick and eight feet long, kept rigidly fixed to the beam above by means of the parallel motion rods. We were able to inspect the 30-foot long cast iron beam at close quarters by going up a second flight of stairs on to the top storey. The floor has a long slot in it to allow space for the beam to move up and down, driven by the piston rod, and access may be had from here on to the balcony which I had seen from below. From this balcony I could see for a great distance, but near at hand I could see all the other buildings in the compound, looking, from that height, like toys; to the north, the cottages of the village, and to the west another mine building, which Mr. Blackwell said was called Carnarvon pit, could be seen. To the south, the rolling country with green fields with cattle quietly grazing and tall trees.

ROADWATER, 1907

'This huge pump, capable of lifting 900 gallons per minute from a depth of six hundred feet, was only built and fixed last year, under Mr. Morgans direction, all in the short space of 10 months,' Mr. Blackwell said proudly as he gave the gleaming valve gear another polish.

'The erection of the engine was very difficult. The cast iron beam, weighing over 20 tons, was hoisted to its present height of 40 feet from the ground without accident of any kind . . .'

We thanked Mr Blackwell and left the pump house.

Of our descent into the bowels of the earth I have little recollection, except of chilly darkness and clammy dampness everywhere. The eerie light cast by the candles stuck with clay to our hats and the distant sound of explosions and smell of powder. Because of the danger, Mr. Morgans could only take us into disused parts of the mine, and so we encountered no miners at work. We climbed up the ladders and for my part, I was very glad to see the sky once more . . .

Later in the afternoon we strolled round the village. It is quite small and was built under Mr. Morgans' direction to provide for all the needs of the miners.

EXTRACTS FROM A BRENDON HILL DIARY, M.H. JONES (1865)

On the south side of the moor, mining had a considerable impact on the communities of North and South Molton. The woodlands on the slopes above North Molton hide several ruined engine houses and mine buildings, and solitary black chimneys stand as memorials to a lost industry. The mines were largely in the valley of the River Mole, around Heasley Mill. The era of greatest prosperity was in the second half of the nineteenth century, although the mines are far older than that, with no definite details known of their origins. However, all activity had ceased by the end of the century and later attempts to restart mining have all been unsuccessful.

DAYS OF RENOWN is the apt title of a small book which recaptures that time of bustle and industry, when the moor was anything but solitary and deserted and the scenery of little or no account – the wealth it could yield was what mattered:

The miners were always to be found in evidence at the local fairs and revels. The villages of this neighbourhood are now quiet and devoid of all the old-time community activity. The North Molton Great Fair (12th November) is now lost and forgotten. This and the May Fair (the first Friday after 11th May) were notable occasions in the social life of North Devon. They had been famous since the day King John gave North Molton to the family of 'de la Zouch'. They were 'never-to-be-forgotten days', the population being increased four and five times with the Square supporting a wonderful collection of country traders who travelled the dusty tracks from as far away as Bristol and Dorchester. There was buying, selling and bartering, accompanied by the amusement sideshows, the music, the dancing, and merry making with plenty to eat and drink. . . .

In August 1856, The North Devon Journal reported that there were great celebrations at Simonsbath on the 18th of the month after the Dowlais Company had reported great expectations from their operations on the Llewellyn lode. Whether this was organised by the Company, or the miners themselves (they were always ready with an excuse for celebration) is not known. . . .

Upon the moor there were George Martin, John White, Henry Scale, William Menelaus and William Dunstan. Scale worked first for the Dowlais Company and then the Plymouth Company. A deeply religious man of enthusiastic temperament he at first impressed but soon disappointed his employers. 'Scale is active and popular' wrote Frederic Knight at one time; and later: 'He is the greatest liar I ever met with.' Among other enterprises, Scale built and operated a shop at Simonsbath at the request of Knight, who was anxious to keep business on the moor instead of benefitting the traders of South Molton. Knight insisted that the prices of the provisions sold be the same as could be bought in South Molton. The shop was kept by Giffard, the innkeeper at Simonsbath, who paid Scale £10 per annum for it.

After the Captain, the most important person in the mine was the Carpenter. Upon him rested the safety of all the others. Hugh Bawden of Heasley Mill was Carpenter at Bampfylde in the 1850s.

BAMPFYLDE COPPER MINE, NORTH MOLTON

His brother Henry was blacksmith (another skilled job) of the same mine. There was John Thorne, Carpenter at Florence in 1857 and William Kingsland, who combined the jobs of carpenter and blacksmith at Bremley, for a long period in the mid-19th century. These were skilled village craftsmen, the like of whom we do not see today.

Billing's Directory and Gazetteer (1875) lists some real characters of the local mining industry. In South Molton there resided Captain William Hall Whitford, inspecting agent for South Molton Silver and Lead Mine (Combe). He was probably a retired Mine Captain. Quite close to him lived Robert Chant, wine and spirit merchant and purser to the Exmoor Wheal Eliza. There is no doubt the two occupations went very well together in catering for the requirements of a copper mine—hard and thirsty work it must have been.

As Mr Slader says, mining must indeed have been thirsty work, and with the closing of the mines many of the inns that served the miners have also gone. Slader describes some of those that have disappeared from the Exmoor scene:

The inns of this neighbourhood have a story of their own, many of them closely linked with the mining industry. Some have disappeared, but others soldier on serving the tourists that visit this beautiful region. Many have now been modernised, sometimes improved in hygiene but not in beauty—stone floored bars with low ceilings and high backed settles have given way to comfortable carpeted lounges. Stables have given way to car parks. Where dim lamps of oil once glowed, there is now bright and glaring strip lighting. In place of the cider and beer barrels, a vast collection of wines, spirits and bottled beers.

In the 1820s, three inns were open on the moor. Of these only The Sportsman at Sandyway has survived. The Red Deer, on the Simonsbath-Exford road, and close to The Picked Stones Mine and Wheal Eliza, is now a farmhouse but in those halcyon days it was known as 'the Gallon House'. Many of Knight's Irish labourers and Welsh miners would gather here and when the shift was over they would often 'down a gallon'. The Acland Arms at Moles Chamber has long since disappeared. It was erected to enable the miners to combat the loneliness of the moor but was not a very reputable house. Being just within the Somerset boundary, it was of course outside the jurisdiction of the neighbouring Devon authorities, while many miles lay between it and the centres of administration in Somerset, and Exmoor, at that time being an extra-parochial district, had no local constable charged with the maintenance of law and order. It is said to have been used as a centre for the distribution of brandy and other smuggled goods landed at various points on the coast between Combe Martin and Porlock. Its position at the intersection of two important packhorse roads must have rendered it a most convenient house for the purpose in the days before carts came into general use.

There has been an inn at Simonsbath since the late 18th century, and even before that Simonsbath Farm was licensed and frequented

NORTH MOLTON

as an inn. In the 19th century The William Rufus Inn (now enlarged and named The Exmoor Forest Hotel) had a wine licence only however. This was at the insistence of Sir Frederic Knight who had a particular dislike of beer. The William Rufus is the inn referred to in 'Lorna Doone' where Tom Faggus was arrested and set free by his strawberry mare.

In North Molton, down towards the River Mole, we come across The Miners' Arms. It has only recently changed hands after being in the same family for 80 years. In the mining era a century ago there were also The Castle, The King's Arms, The Poltimore Arms, The Swan, and The Somerset. On pay nights, after work ceased at the local mines, they remained open all night and were generally full into the early morning. The present Poltimore Arms was two separate houses owned by Lord Poltimore until about 1840. Previous to that, the inn bearing this name was in the present estate office at the north of the Square. This was known as The Bampfylde Arms early in the 19th century. It changed its name in 1831 when Sir George Bampfylde was created Lord Poltimore.

At Molland we cannot help but notice The London Inn, close by the church, surrounded by beautiful creatures of the moor – the red deer, the foxes, the badgers, and the owl. The London however was famous long before its miniature zoo. Beneath the low ceilings, in the days when they brewed their own ale, the bar for long echoed the voices of the miners of Bremley. The Buckingham family has kept The London for three generations.

DAYS OF RENOWN, J.M. SLADER (1965)

Of a completely different nature were the silver mines of Combe Martin, by far the oldest on the moor:

In the reign of Edward I., 337 men were brought out of Derbyshire to work the silver mines at this place. They are said to have been at that period very productive, and to have furnished money for the wars in the reign of Edward III. They were again worked with success in the reign of Queen Elizabeth, by Sir Beavis

RUINS OF MINE BUILDINGS, COMBE MARTIN

Bulmer. About twenty years ago, an unsuccessful attempt was made to work these mines: they were again opened in 1817, and worked to some extent; but the produce was not such as to reward the adventurers for their exertions, and the work has been abandoned.

TOPOGRAPHICAL AND HISTORICAL ACCOUNT OF DEVONSHIRE,

REVD D. LYSON (1822)

All activity had long since ceased when Mr J.L.W. Page came across the old mines, but his description gives some idea of their nature, and of the hardships endured by those early miners:

Overhead, dark against the sky, towers the Great Hangman the loftiest seaward hill in the West of England. The climb to the summit, say, from the point where Sherracombe opens on to the sea, is nearly a thousand feet, for the Great Hangman is 1044 feet high. So it is mountaineering now with a vengeance. I have done some of the worst of the Lake mountains, I have done Ben Nevis, but I know nothing, except perhaps the screes of Rosset Ghyll, to equal the tremendous climb up the slippery slopes of the Great Hangman. The gradient is about one in two, and you will find it necessary to pause very frequently under colour of admiring the view over the ravine below.

About three hundred feet from the summit an old mine track leads outwards and along the face past the chasm inside Blackstone Point to some adits tunnelled in the days when these hills were worked for silver, lead, iron, and copper. The first opening is a mere pit, but the second discloses the entrance to two passages or tunnels. The first, a steep and loose descent underground, dives into a short passage, which, turning sharp to the right, opens suddenly on the face of a precipice some seven hundred feet high. In the roof is a round hole which lets down a little light. The mineral was doubtless hauled up the shaft, the refuse being tipped into the sea below. The tunnel to the left passes into the hill for a distance of one hundred and fifty feet.

Beneath the track is an overgrown path running obliquely nearly to the edge of the cliff, where we come upon another tunnel, striking for about ninety feet in a direct line into the hill, and then branching to the left. Its greatest length, from the window-like opening in the cliff to the end, is one hundred and ten paces, or, say, three hundred and thirty feet. None of these passages are more than about three feet wide and about seven feet high.

Half a mile beyond—to the westward—a zigzag path descends a sloping part of the cliff to the beach. It is now used by people to collect driftwood and laver from the rocks. Laver, by the way, is a seaweed which is boiled and eaten very much in the same way as spinach, which in appearance it somewhat resembles. But in the old mining days this path had other uses, for about forty feet above the beach are two more caves. They have long been abandoned, and could never, one would think, have been very productive, for no cart could by any possibility have ascended the face of the cliff, and the mineral must have been carried up in baskets. A little further west a path, cut in the cliff, leads to another adit which has been filled up (apparently by a fall from the roof) just within the entrance.

THE COASTS OF DEVON, J.L.W. PAGE (1895)

An early view of Combe Martin comes from W.G. Maton in 1797, when visitors were few, and providing for them as yet formed no part of the economy of the village:

The sea enters a little cove at Combe-Martin, commodious for the mooring of small vessels; and here the produce of the mines is shipped for Wales and Bristol. The manor of this village, Gibson says, in the reign of Henry I. belonged to *Martin* de Tours, a Norman baron, from whom, I guess, the latter part of its name must have been derived.—There is no curiosity, in the way of antiquities, except an old manor-house. This building, by its ruinous aspect, freshens the melancholy with which we are accustomed to reflect on the decline of the honest hospitality of our fore-fathers, and added to the romantic aspect of the scenery around, the seclusion of the spot, and its remoteness from any other spectacles than those of purely rural life, awakens emotions that minds of a contemplative turn love to indulge.—The mansion has long been deserted by its proprietors,

COMBE MARTIN

and, though still tenanted by a farmer, approaches the last stage of decay.—This village affords none but the most coarse accommodations,—a circumstance which we regretted as being likely to deter travellers of more nicety than curiosity or enthusiasm from bestowing on this charming spot the attention it might otherwise command from them.

Observations of the Western Counties of England, Wm G. Maton (1794)

By 1939 things had much improved as Combe Martin took advantage of the rapidly developing holiday trade. The population quoted in the Ward Lock Red Guide for that year is given as about 2,000: it doubled in summer!:

Combe Martin, situated amid delightful scenery, has developed greatly in the last few years and has become very popular as a holiday centre. The name is derived from *combe*—'a low and deep valley surrounded by very high hills,' and *Martin*—'Le Sieur Martin de Tours,' a man of much worth and assistance to William Duke of Normandy, whose name is also perpetuated in the village of Martinhoe. The view from the hill on the Ilfracombe side of the bay is charming. Green fields, well-cultivated market gardens, quaint cottages and pleasant houses make a comfortable picture contrasting well with the wild scenery of the coast.

The little bay, tucked away among the cliffs, is picturesque at all times, and at low water the stream meanders seawards across the sands, but the visitor should heed warning notices about the danger of falling cliffs, as these falls occur from time to time. Overlooking the bay on the west side, and shaded by trees in part, is the **Pleasure Ground**, provided with seats. It is the best place in Combe Martin to watch the wonderful sea and sky effects, which are especially beautiful towards evening, when the setting sun deepens and strengthens the colour contrasts of the land.

The village consists principally of a single long, straggling street, more than a mile and a half in length, nearly all on the incline and just wide enough for two buses to pass one another. To the lover of quiet, the place is an ideal holiday resort, and is an excellent centre for motoring, cycling and walking. There are good shops, houses which are let furnished during the summer months, and numerous houses in which rooms are let to visitors.

The climate of this charming place has been described as almost perfect. The winter scarcely ever starts before January. The rain runs off the high hills, and the soil being shale, gravel and rock, paths dry quickly. The air is mild and would be relaxing were it not for the sea breezes which blow from the north-west and seem to come straight from the Atlantic. A stay at Combe Martin is often recommended for patients threatened with lung trouble, and it is popular with those who have lived long in the Tropics, many of whom choose to retire in the neighbourhood.

Market-gardening and fruit-growing are important local industries, the soil and climate being very favourable, and the produce finding a ready sale in Ilfracombe, Lynton and Lynmouth. Many tons of strawberries are dispatched to London, South Wales, and other large centres in the early summer. In spring the fields of daffodils are like sheets of fairy gold.

Red Guide, Ward Lock (1911)

Many writers on Exmoor ignore the far western heights between Lynmouth and Combe Martin, and miss some magnificent scenery in so doing. Not so the indefatigable Mr Page. He journeyed on from the Great Hangman, even risking his neck on the way to Heddon's Mouth. In his day there was no well-defined coastal footpath for the walker to follow!

Heddon's Mouth and the Hunters Inn are popular tourist meccas. The inn is no longer thatched, having been burnt down not long after Mr Page's visit:

Sweeping out once more on to the face of the cliffs, the path winds onwards, now over grass, now across screes—a dangerous walk at night, for, once lose your balance, and you fall, or, rather, roll, many hundred feet, and then—annihilation. At one point we pass close to the brink, and look right down on the sea. There are many caves at the foot of these cliffs, and some are accessible by the zigzag path cut by Bishop Hannington between Hollow Brook Combe and

HUNTER'S INN

Heddon's Mouth. But this path does not look tempting, and I cannot say that I should like to try such a descent.

And now a bold, rough ridge of rocks cuts the western sky line, sinking at a sharp angle to the sea—High Veer. The path is hewn through the upper end, and, as we pass through, almost without warning opens out the valley of Heddon's Mouth, thought, by more than one, to be the finest of the combes of North Devon. We look down upon the trout stream flashing seaward towards the bar of shingle which the sea has piled across its mouth, and through which it must filter, save when a storm on the moors sends down a flood, when, for a brief space, the barrier gives way. An abandoned limekiln perched on the rocky bank overlooks the struggle between stream and sea, and, worn by age and the weather to picturesqueness, is like some old castle guarding the pass inland.

The valley is shut in by lofty hills. On the western side the stone-strewn slopes give to the scene an air of grand desolation. In the glare of mid-day the effect is not so imposing, but it is difficult to do justice to it at sunset. With the light at their back, the hills turn a deep blue purple, while the screes become a pinkish grey, and over all spreads a pale mist, so transparent as scarce to be mist at all. Up from the depths below come glints of light where, here and there, the Heddon curls back against a boulder, and the air is full of his voice, rising to this height in soft undertone.

But, even at mid-day, the glen is beautiful. And look at the colouring—that burning bush of gorse bursting forth from the arid stretch of stone—there is yellow, and pink, and grey. A few months distant, and the clump of heather on the edge of that fern brake will be in full bloom, and the bracken itself changing its tints beneath the breath of autumn—then will there be purple and gold. And everywhere in and out among the rocks are there bright green patches of moss and blades of grass.

And now the path passes downwards almost to the bank of the river and through a wood to the Hunters' Inn, a picturesque thatched hostelry at the foot of wooded heights, in the fork where the main stream is joined by a brook coming down another deep valley from the cultivated country at the back of Trentishoe. Both streams are full of trout, so the Hunters' Inn is a favourite headquarters for fishermen. It is also much affected by 'reading men,' and the young man from Oxford may often be seen sunning himself on the seat in front, engaged in the perusal of some work which does not *look* a bit classical. But then they bind books oddly nowadays, and perhaps a yellow cover makes Plato or Thucydides more attractive, while, as everyone knows, it does not follow that because a book is in three volumes and has the purple label of Smith it is not sternly scholastic.

A road of true West Country steepness and stoniness climbs the western combe to Trentishoe Church and what there is of a hamlet—a farm and a cottage or two. The church, although on such high ground, is well sheltered by still higher land behind, as well as by a grove of ash trees which rise above the low tower. It is a tiny building with an Early English east window of three lights. Here, as at Martinhoe, the churchyard affords examples of primitive epitaphs, one of which, commencing

> My lovely little Tommy,
> Thou was taken very soon,

has 'angles' for 'angels,' and 'nown' for 'known.'

But in spite of bad spelling—or perhaps because of it—people seem to live long at Trentishoe. On one gravestone we find that three people, all bearing the ancient and timehonoured patronymic of Jones, lived to be 89, 92, and 103 respectively. There is no doubt that people do live long in these peaceful out-of-the-way spots. A tourist once met an old man sobbing bitterly. 'Why do you cry, my man?' he asked. 'Feyther hev a been beating me,' blubbered the old fellow. 'Father been beating you?' echoed the astonished wayfarer. 'What on earth for?' 'For throwing stones at gran'feyther,' whined the veteran.

THE COASTS OF DEVON, J.L.W. PAGE (1895)

ELEVEN

Sporting Exmoor

Creatures of the wild are often dependent on man — sometimes their worst enemy, often their preserver and best friend. This passage demonstrates how two of Exmoor's best-known animals owe their continued survival to the hand of man — the red deer and the Exmoor pony:

Mr. Knight, afterwards Sir Frederick, was in the habit of spending a couple of months or so every autumn at the quaint, rambling house, like a coaching inn with its front door, upon the high road, at Simonsbath. It had formerly been the old Crown Lodge of the Forest, when the latter was Crown property, before the days of Mr. Knight's over-enterprising father. Our Mr. Knight had an only son of about our age, who died young, a misfortune which, I believe, influenced his father, being also a large landowner in Worcestershire, in selling the reversion of Exmoor later on to the Fortescue family. When the son was at home we were occasionally asked to shoot with him over his better-keeper'd domain around Simonsbath, which marched with ours, but where black game was rather more plentiful than on our side of the boundary.

Since those days many of the wild hills, which then carried heather, and the bottoms that quaked with bog have been ditched, limed and drained, larch and fir woods planted on the hill-sides, and even the plough, I am told, now runs in many places where of yore the nesting curlew trilled and the heath poults hatched their broods. Sometimes, too, on these occasions we would dine at the Manor House with its kind host. He had a rather special interest for us, having been in his day reputed one of the hardest riders after the stag-hounds, together with Jack Russell, Dr. Collyns, and other notables. Apropos of the Knight brothers, Mr. Russell tells a story somewhere

of Limpetty, first Mr. Trelawny's huntsman at South Molton and afterwards with Mr. Fenwick Bisset of stag-hound fame. He was a desperate rider when his blood was up, and on this occasion, when in the air, over the biggest and most dangerous water jump the famous parson had ever seen him face, he turned his head and called out defiantly: 'Where be they Knights tew now I should like to knaw.'

Mr. Frederick Knight's handsome and stately lady, as in memory she comes back to me, had also a particular interest for us lads from having been flung with her carriage and horses down the steep gorge of the East Lynn that we knew so well, and escaping I think, uninjured.

We saw very little of the stag-hounds on our side of the moor in those days. They had, of course, nothing approaching the fields and spectators of recent times. Indeed, a dozen or so years previously the pack had, I believe, almost collapsed, and the deer had dwindled to a few score all told. Under Mr. Fenwick Bisset, however, the stock had greatly increased and the hunting had improved with rapid strides, but comparatively few strangers, I fancy, came down even then to ride with them, and as there were very few tourists at that time in the neighbouring sea coast villages, and none at all on any part of the moor, that we at least had knowledge of, there was nothing approaching the crowd of onlookers that now foregather at the earlier meets. Indeed, we very seldom had a sight of any deer on our side. For one thing, there was very little harbourage for breeding on Exmoor forest proper, or in our parish. What woods there were had for the most part been recently planted. Occasionally, but not often, there was a run into or through our country. I remember in one of these, a stag was hunted through Paracombe parish and down to Combe Martin, where, having run all down the mile-long village street, heading for the sea, it was coolly shot on the beach by the village policeman, off duty at the moment and in quest of sea birds. That hapless and dunder-headed official had a terrible time, it was said, when the hunt arrived upon the scene, and for quite a long time afterwards wished that he had never been born.

There was always in those days an abundance of ponies on the hills around Simonsbath. For the first Mr. Knight, among all his other enterprises, had been a great breeder of the Exmoor pony. The Acland family, who belonged to the further bounds of the forest, were the other and older patrons of the breed. These shaggy little brutes, of but eleven to twelve hands in the pure strain, had run wild over the moor in hundreds in the eighteenth century, not ownerless, of course, but almost as *ferae naturae*. Just after Waterloo nearly all the ponies on the moor had been collected, sold by auction and shipped to various parts. Sir Thomas Acland reserved a score or so of the best and bred henceforward the pure and smaller strain. Mr. Knight got hold of another bunch, and here at Simonsbath bred, from a small Arab stallion, a larger type, which appears to have lost the native powers of facing the winters on the moor without artificial keep. But I fancy by the 'sixties the Simonsbath herds had reverted a good deal to type and took what the gods sent them on the wintry moor. They were rough enough little brutes in all conscience, brown or bay in colour, and while being corralled into the yards at Simonsbath for sorting, branding or other purposes, a procedure I witnessed more than once, described antics beside which an old-fashioned Rugby football scrimmage would have seemed a minuet. Large drafts from all over the moor used to be driven to Bampton Fair annually and dispersed to destinations as various as carrying a duke's son in Rotten Row and working at the bottom of a coal mine in South Wales—a sorry shift this last from galloping about the Exmoor hills.

The snows of winter have in truth no terrors for the pony when inured to them. The horses used to come well out of the fierce winters of North-Western Canada when cattle were dying by hundreds,

before winter feeding was introduced. What the origin of these mountain ponies, whether of Exmoor, Dartmoor or Wales, is a popular subject of speculation. Degenerate horses no doubt. For centuries of rough weather and poor feeding must surely tend to such effect.

EXMOOR MEMORIES, A.G. BRADLEY (1926)

A fuller description of the preservation and development of the Exmoor breed comes from Sabine Baring-Gould's A BOOK OF THE WEST:

An after-dinner conversation led Mr. Knight to consider the great pony question in all its bearings. The party met at Sir Joseph Banks's, the eminent naturalist. They discussed the merits of the Dongola horse, which had been described as an Arab of sixteen hands and peculiar to the regions round Nubia. Sir Joseph proposed to the party to get some of the breed, and accordingly Lords Headly, Morton, and Dundas, and Mr. Knight then and there gave him a joint £1000 cheque as a deposit for the expenses. The English consul in Egypt was applied to, and in due course the horses and mares which he sent bore out Bruce's description to the letter. In addition to their height, they were rather Roman-nosed, with a very fine texture of skin, well chiselled under the jowl, and as clean-winded as all their race. About ten or twelve arrived, and Mr. Knight was so pleased with them that he bought Lord Headly's share. His two sires and three mares were then brought to Simonsbath, where he had established a stud of seven or eight thoroughbred mares and thirty half-breeds of the coaching Cleveland sort.

The first cross knocked out the Roman nose as completely as the Leicester destroys the Exmoor horn, but the buffy stood true to its colour, and thus the type was never quite lost. The half Dongolas did wonderfully well with the West Somerset, which often came to Exmoor to draw for a fox, and they managed to get down the difficult hills so well, and crossed the brooks so close up with the hounds, that the vocation of the white-clad guides on chase days gradually fell into disuse.

The average height is $12\frac{1}{2}$ hands, and bays and buffy bays with mealy noses prevail; in fact, are in a majority of at least three to one.

THE STAG THE HARBOURER WANTS TO FIND

Exmoor and the red deer are synonymous – indeed, a stag's head was chosen as the emblem of the Exmoor National Park.

Even in his short life Richard Jefferies managed to gain a considerable reputation as an observer of the countryside, a naturalist and champion of rural life. He wrote RED DEER, gaining much help from one of the foremost huntsmen of the day and his son, Fred and Arthur Heal. It remains a classic work:

Besides being his weapons of offence the horns to some extent are the stag's armour. As he starts he throws his head well back and the horns fit each side of his neck or shoulder, and so guard him from the thick thorn bushes into which he often plunges. Young hounds sometimes seize the antler, but quickly leave hold. The new horns . . . begin to grow with the brake fern, and the velvet is rubbed off towards the end of July, or beginning of August, so that they take four months to come to this complete state. At the same time the hart or stag sheds his coat, and in June appears in his full red-gold colour.

In October again, as the stag-hunting ceases, the horns are employed in fighting, the stags then combating for their lady-loves. The life of a stag is indeed so bound up with the growth and condition of his antlers that it may be said to begin and end with them. Before they are high enough to be dignified as horns the young male deer runs with the hinds and herds with them. There is little difference in their appearance, and it sometimes happens in the hind-hunting season that a young male deer is chased for some time till the mistake is discovered. The outline of the face is broader and shorter—a hind's face looks longer—and by this the heads may be distinguished. As he grows older, and the antlers each season become larger, the deer leaves the hinds and joins the stags, feeding and harbouring in company with one of them. At last a full-grown stag, he is in his turn master, and has a companion, as it were, to fag for him. In his old age the antlers each year diminish in points and size, the beam becomes thinner, and from four on top the points dwindle to three, and then to two, so as to look like those of a young stag.

The older ponies live all through the winter on the hills, and seek out sheltered spots for themselves during the continuance of wind and rain. These favourite nooks are well known to the herdsmen, who build up stacks of hay and straw, which are doled out to them in times of snow. 'Still, like honest, hard-working labourers, the ponies never assemble at the wicket till they have exhausted every means of self-support by scratching with their fore-feet in the snow for the remnants of the summer tufts, and drag wearily behind them an ever lengthening chain of snowballs.

A BOOK OF THE WEST, S. BARING-GOULD (1899)

There is no more beautiful creature than a stag in his pride of antler, his coat of ruddy gold, his grace of form and motion. He seems the natural owner of the ferny coombes, the oak woods, the broad slopes of heather. They belong to him, and he steps upon the sward in lordly mastership. The land is his, and the hills, the sweet streams, and rocky glens. He is infinitely more natural than the cattle and sheep that have strayed into his domains. For some inexplicable reason, although they too are in reality natural, when he is present they look as if they had been put there and were kept there by artificial means. They do not, as painters say, shade in with the colours and shape of the landscape. He is as natural as an oak, or a fern, or a rock itself. He is earth-born—autochthon—and holds possession by descent. Utterly scorning control, the walls and hedges are nothing to him—he roams where he chooses, as fancy leads, and gathers the food that pleases him.

Pillaging the crops and claiming his dues from the orchards and gardens, he exercises his ancient feudal rights, indifferent to the laws of house-people. Disturb him in his wild stronghold of oak wood or heather, and, as he yields to force, still he stops and looks back proudly. He is slain, but never conquered. He will not cross with the tame park deer; proud as a Spanish noble, he disdains the fallow deer, and breeds only with his own race. But it is chiefly because of his singular adaptation and fitness to the places where he is found that he obtains our sympathy.

Most writers unite in their admiration of the beauty and nobility of the stag. Yet Jefferies' account of the destructive feeding habits of the deer help to explain why stag hunting is such a feature of moorland life. It is interesting to note that, while there have always been keen naturalists and lovers of wildlife, none of them appear to have been against the hunt, and certainly to country folk it was – and still is – an accepted part of life.

These deer have been hitherto spoken of as the red deer of Exmoor, but they have now extended so widely, roaming over great tracts of two counties, that this limited term is no longer applicable. They are now the red deer of the West of England. But Exmoor was

their retreat during the long, long passage of time down from mediaeval days to our own, and it was from thence that they spread abroad under favourable conditions. It remains the centre of Red Deer Land, and without a clear idea of this remarkable district no one can comprehend how it is that the deer are so really wild.

The moors of the Exe river are not flat stretches of marshland, but hills of great height covered with heather. The term mountains may almost be applied to them—numbers of the ridges are twice the height of Beachy Head or the Dyke at Brighton—Dunkery Beacon is three times as high. But the conformation of the country is such that on entering it the elevations do not seem very unusual, for as it is all high and raised the eye has nothing with which to contrast it. When on the moor it appears an immense table-land, intersected by deep narrow valleys, called coombes, at the bottom of which a stream always flows. At some distance apart are ranges of hills rising gradually and with gentle slopes above the general level of the moor. The curves appear so moderate and the ascent so easy that there can be no difficulty in walking or riding over them. Dunkery itself is nothing more than an undulation, scarcely to be separated at some points of view from the common line of the ridge. These hills seem only a mile or two away and within half-an-hour's walk.

But on going towards them, the table-land suddenly sinks in a deep coombe, when it is apparent that the moor which looked so level is really the top of a hill. This coombe has to be descended, and ascended, and the sides are high and steep. Presently another coombe intervenes, and after five miles' walking very little progress has been made. At last the slope of the hill is reached, and has now expanded into a mountainous ascent, not to be overcome without much labour and more time. The country is, in fact, very deceptive, much wider, and much more difficult than it looks. The expanse confuses the eye, and will not allow it to judge distances. From the spot where you stand to the range yonder is perhaps five-and-twenty miles. On Haddon Hill the glance passes from Dunkery, which overlooks the Severn Sea, to Sidmouth Gap by St. George's Channel, so that the eye sees across the entire breadth of England there.

The consequence of these great distances is that all minor distances are shrunken, and five miles looks nothing. The illusion is assisted by the smooth outline of the moors, without a fence for miles together, and without a visible tree, for the covers are in the coombes, and there are few or no copses on the hills, as in the South Downs. Nothing whatever breaks up the surface and measures the view. Heather covers the largest part of the ground, which is never ploughed or sown, and where there are no flower-grown meads. One vast breadth of open, wild, and treeless country reaches in every direction, and it is at once obvious why the deer have remained at large since the most ancient times, for the land is in the same condition as it was centuries ago. The plough has not touched it, and civilisation has not come near.

RED DEER, RICHARD JEFFERIES (1884)

CLOUTSHAM FARM

The land is no longer in the same condition as it was centuries ago. Much of the heather has disappeared under the plough, but the deep, wooded combes of which Jefferies speaks remain and are still the haunt of the deer. But the red deer are no longer found throughout the West Country; they have retreated to what may well prove to be their last stronghold, south of the Border.

Hunting itself has changed little over the centuries and, should the traditional methods be superseded so that the stag has less than a fair chance, then hunting will have sounded its own death knell. It is the traditionalists who support it and the traditionalists who defend it. But the nature of the hunt followers has changed dramatically since these accounts of one of the most famous of meets, that at Cloutsham Ball:

Much has been written, and that by many an able pen, of the great annual gathering that takes place on a little rounded hill-top between Dunkery and the fertile vale of Holnicote, when for one day, at least, in all the year 'everybody who is anybody' within half a county's length makes picnic upon this spot that has seen the Devon and Somerset Staghounds in all their glory from such time as the memory of living man runneth not to the contrary. One of the chief reasons of the unfailing popularity of the opening meet is doubtless to be found in the fact that it affords the very first opportunity after the enforced idleness of summer for the foregathering of all the various sorts and conditions of men that go to make up a modern hunting field. Then, too, nearly every master of foxhounds throughout the British Isles is as yet free from the cares of cub-hunting, and many of them wend their way to Cloutsham, where they are sure of meeting a number of their confrères. A sprinkling of American visitors are sure to be found amongst the throng by the time the pack appears, some of them tourists only, who have chanced to find themselves at Lynton or Lynmouth, or perhaps at Minehead, just at the time of this great West Country festival, and others members of Hunt Clubs in the land of the star-spangled banner. Austrians and Russians, Belgians and Germans, Frenchmen, Portuguese and Spaniards are at times to be found amongst the throng, and occasionally a 'coloured pusson' or two join in the first mad rush of the season. . . .

Many a portent has arisen at the opening meets; a white Spanish mule has been ridden, not only into the meeting field, but also after the hounds; a German band, with brazen instruments and uniforms complete, has applied in vain for admission, for, be it remembered, the historic field and the farm and all its surroundings are private property, and are only thrown open to the Hunt and its many followers by the courtesy of the owner, Sir C.T.D. Acland. Many a four-in-hand has braved successfully the perils of the mountain roads, and every sort of char-a-banc and brake brings its contribution of foot people to swell the throng. Some cyclists laboriously wheel their machines up the last long ascent from Horner, while others more wisely leave them in safe keeping below and climb the remaining distance unencumbered. Breakdowns and minor accidents are plentiful, but not more so than one might expect, having regard to the difficulties of the way and the curious collection of vehicles and tackle pressed into the day's service.

A few years since a newly-married barrister and his bride had the misfortune to break a leg a-piece in a carriage accident of this description, and a little later on were to be seen attending the meets on wheels, duly strapped and splinted and were naturally the recipients of unstinted sympathy. . . .

The time of the year being mid-August, it is not surprising that there is a great diversity of opinion as to the most suitable attire for the occasion, and inasmuch as the Hunt uniform is worn only by the master and two servants and the honorary secretary and by Lord Ebrington on certain days, all that has to be attained is a garb sufficiently cool and at the same time serviceable. Straw hats of any rigid shape are undoubtedly a mistake, as they invariably blow off directly business begins. Many ladies wear light coats of white drill, and one enterprising sportsman attired himself in a spotless suit of duck not many summers ago, and was promptly set down in the columns of the *Sporting Times* as 'one clad in white samite.' A few khaki garments were in evidence amongst the field in the summer of 1900, and a certain number of invalided troopers with uniform and cowboy hats complete were to be seen.

STAGHUNTING WITH THE DEVON AND SOMERSET, PHILIP EVERED (1902)

The regular trysting place (of the Devon & Somerset Staghounds) was on Cloutsham Ball and the event never fails to attract a huge mob of picnickers who arrive from every point of the compass in wagonettes, drags, dogcarts etc. usually requisitioned at Dulverton, Dunster, Minehead and other centres several days in advance, spreading themselves in picturesque groups round white cloths they may be seen quaffing their cider or champagne, and discussing their ham and chicken full of animation at the prospect of witnessing the sport, where everywhere you hear the kindly Westcountry drawl as friends exchange greetings.

BOOK OF EXMOOR, F.J. SNELL (1903)

The other side of the coin is displayed in this wicked little anecdote of hunting on a wet day!:

When it rains here it does it well and truly, and *a propos* of this I once saw a rare comic scene on a stag hunt meet a few years ago on the top of Hawkcombe Head. A lady from India had come out hunting in a tropical riding habit and one of Exmoor's showers quickly converted this into a skintight covering for her rather fully-blown figure. In a few moments it left her looking very like a buxom Lady Godiva on her grey horse, but unfortunately for her, without that Coventry lady's flowing tresses. One can get wetter on Exmoor on a rainy day, or when a cold drenching fog covers the hills, than in any other place in England.

EXMOOR: THE RIDING PLAYGROUND OF ENGLAND, CECIL ALDIN (1935)

The most famous meet of all, unlikely ever to be matched in these days of anti-hunting groups, was when the Prince of Wales graced Exmoor. Strange to say, although Exmoor was a Royal Chase until 1819, no royal personage ever hunted here; it took Parson Jack Russell to change that:

What a day that was on Exmoor, that August day of 1879, when the Prince of Wales attended the meet of the staghounds on Hawkcombe Head!

Just imagine the excitement in the neighbourhood, and for miles far around, when the news was bruited abroad that the Prince would

LORD POLTIMORE AT TWITCHEN WITH MR THORNE AND HOUNDS

PUPPY JUDGING AT NORTH MOLTON

be present at the opening meet of the Devon and Somerset Staghounds!

No prince had visited Exmoor since young Prince Charles (later Charles II) had fled across Exmoor, with some faithful attendants, from Dunster Castle to Barnstaple to escape the Roundheads.

Perhaps no royal personage had hunted the deer on Exmoor since Edward, Duke of York, nephew of John of Gaunt and cousin of Henry V, came to Somerset as 'Master of Game' in the year 1396. Yet Somerset was a famous hunting-ground for Saxon and Norman kings for many hundreds of years.

Those who were in the secret told how the dearest wish of Parson Jack Russell had been to bring the Prince of Wales to Exmoor, and thereby stir a wider interest in this noble sport of staghunting to the benefit of the west country. On the subject of his favourite sport, staghunting, Russell would hold his hearers spellbound. The Prince's imagination was fired—was he not a true sportsman! The happy result was this promised visit to the west country. West country folk have a gift of rising to the occasion and prepared to give the Prince a true Exmoor welcome. But alas! Fate stepped in and threatened ruin to their hopes. Within a few months of the visit, hydrophobia broke out again in the kennels and the pack had to be destroyed.

The effect of this stunning blow on the countryside can be imagined. Could a new pack, fit to hunt the deer in time-honoured fashion, be raised in time? Many said it was hopeless and the visit must be cancelled. One man never doubted it could be done, and on him rested the sole responsibility of doing it—Arthur Heal! Despite all doubts and fears the master and committee trusted him. If any man in England could do the impossible, Arthur Heal could do it! The committee, to the joy of the whole country, decided to 'carry on'! The story of how that miracle was accomplished, despite all fears and setbacks, has already been told. We come now to its eventual, triumphant success.

The great day of the meet broke gloriously fine, after a night of heavy rain over Exmoor. There was no doubt but that the weather would contribute to the success of this momentous day in the annals of staghunting.

No sooner had the sun risen over the hills than grooms were busy feeding and dressing their horses in every village within thirty miles of the meet. Long ere the sun's rays shone down on heather and whortleberry and fern, now glistening with raindrops, little parties were wending their way from places as far apart as Barnstaple, Tiverton, Dulverton, Minehead, and Taunton, to the trysting-place overlooking the Bristol Channel at Hawkcombe Head. . . .

The scene on Hawkcombe Head beggars description! Mrs. Benfield, a well-known follower of the hounds, then a young girl, thought 10,000 people were present. 'Dragon', an experienced judge of large crowds, puts the figure at 15,000 or over. He estimates that 1,200 or 1,500 were mounted. . . .

Hounds were kennelled as usual at Culbone Stables. Then followed the calling out of the tufters, three couple of hounds, including, we may be sure, the few saved from the old pack. They will be sorely needed to-day! The harbourer and huntsman ride off with the tufters, and are lost in the big fir plantations. The immense throng of onlookers spreads itself over the heather on either side of the roads prepared to enjoy the morning.

The first thing noticeable on the Moor when hounds are drawing is the silence. Voices remain subdued or are lost in the great silence. The voice of the huntsman, encouraging a hound in the distance, rising clear and distinct, emphasizes rather than breaks the stillness.

The Prince was sitting his horse, in the midst of a group of farmers, eating bread and cheese. A space was kept around him by a few sportsmen, among them that veteran staghunter, Mr. Joyce. 'I've kept the ring many times for wrestling matches,' he remarked, laughing, 'but never before for a prince!'

Just then a true west country diversion occurred. A rider rode into the sacred circle, quite unabashed, and approached the Prince. He was in his shirt-sleeves, wearing corduroy trousers tied at the knee, and boots muddy from the plough. His horse had evidently done a morning's ploughing in the fields nearby.

'Good morning, Mister Purnce!' said the farmer, touching his cap.

'Good morning, farmer!' replied the Prince, smiling.

'Thick be a vine 'oss thee'm riding, Mr. Purnce,' said the famer, after casting an expert eye over the Prince's mount.

The Prince (delighted): 'Yes, farmer! Where do you think I bought him?'

The farmer: 'Can't zay, Mr Purnce.'

'Out of a butcher's cart in Southampton!' said the Prince.

'Then, thee'm a better judge of 'osses than I be, Mister Purnce!' replied the farmer. With that, with the natural courtesy of a true west countryman, he touched his cap and disappeared in the throng. . . .

Soon it becomes apparent to those in charge of the day's proceedings that no stag will be roused that day to face the crowds that throng the hill. However, no one grudges them their fun. The time has not been lost which has afforded so great a pleasure to so vast a throng. Mr. Snow has safely harboured a warrantable stag in Badgworthy in anticipation of just such an event. So the order is given for Badgworthy.

While the hunt moves on to the deer park, we can pause to ask who had the responsible task of piloting the Prince? Claud Luttrell says—Earl Fortescue. Harry Lock, then a boy driven up by his parents from Oare, says Mr. Chorley. In Porlock another story was current, too racy to be omitted. According to Porlock tradition, the pilots were Parson Jack Russell and Mr. Snow.

Close by the deer park fence an innocent-looking hollow of grass and rushes encroaches into the heather. When the Prince and his pilots arrived on the spot, the two pilots, moved by some mutual understanding, suddenly drew apart. The Prince rode on. His horse sank into the mire. He was bogged!

A farmer on the spot remarked to the Prince, now clasping his horse round the neck: 'Dirty going here about, Mr Purnce!'

The horse plunged through. It was only a little one! The Prince retained his seat. All was well! But the Prince had been well and truly bogged to the delight of all the Field, no less than to that prince of sportsmen, the Prince himself. . . .

The stag was duly raised over at Badgworthy, and chased to the finish. The account recalls how the Prince himself was asked to despatch the beast, and did so with skill and nerve which were the subject of much discussion between the Prince and Arthur Heal. Apparently the Prince learnt his method in Scotland and ever after, so the chronicler tells us, this has been adopted on Exmoor. But there was an interesting end to the tale—

That evening, Claud Luttrell tells us, a strange, disturbing rumour was abroad in the streets and clubs of London that the Prince had committed suicide!

A reporter had telegraphed an account of the day, and ended his report with the cryptic words:

'The stag was killed in the Doone valley. The Prince cut his throat!'

EXMOOR, SPORTING & OTHERWISE, H.J. MARSHALL (1948)

Many interesting stories concerning Exmoor are to be found in two small volumes, ECHOES OF EXMOOR. These purport to be the annals of a distinguished and secret club, described in the introduction:

There is in one of the old market towns bordering on the Moors an ancient club of Exmoor men. One of its chief glories is that its formation goes back to the days when the Forest belonged to the King. It is held that it had its birth among the ancient King's Foresters or else their successors, who inaugurated and ran the 'Exmoor Hunt' after the deforestation. This takes us back to the times of the Commonwealth and immediately after. The original purpose of the club (so the tradition says) was to put down and exterminate the savage Doones, whose exploits were the terror of the neighbourhood. It was therefore necessarily a secret club. Very few of its members were known to the neighbourhood by name, for fear of its purposes being overthrown by gossip, and this secretive character has been fairly well preserved down to the present time. It is an unwritten rule that its members shall not be mentioned by name until they have passed away.

To this club belonged in later times the renowned Parson Jack Russell and his notorious brother, Jack Froude. With the movement

HOUNDS CROSSING NORTH MOLTON BRIDGE

of time the superficials of this institution have naturally altered, but these things only add abiding loyalty and pride to its membership and zeal to its officials. At this club I shall often be found (if you can discern my identity), and in the town, especially on market days.

It is from these tales that this anecdote of Parson Jack Russell comes. Just why he should have been such a favourite of the royal couple is not clear, but that he was seems obvious from the following:

I was also reading the other day an autobiography of a nobleman who met Russell at Sandringham, and I came across this note about him: 'A unique sort of elderly cleric from the West of England was present at the dinner—the Rev John Russell—who talked incessantly with a broad accent and a touch of dialect. Both the Prince and Princess seemed absorbed in his conversation, whom he addressed in the homeliest fashion consistent with gentle courtesy. The other guests were drawn in as listeners, our faces beaming and our feelings tickled as he blended 'my dearr' (to the Princess!) and 'me zin' (to the Prince) with a mixture of 'Yer Highness' and 'Sir' or 'Madam' in his address. His complacency is clearly born of simplicity, and so is more than bereft of offence.

It has often been asked amongst us what it was in Russell besides his fine sporting temper, and his manly defence of it in the form of Hunting, that commended him to Prince Albert Edward, for surely the Prince had many chances of meeting this quality in the multitudes of Englishmen that possess it in abundance—except that few of them could be found in the ranks of the Clergy. It may therefore have been this rare, curious, and yet healthy combination that singled him out for distinction. There is, however, a tradition at the Club, that he was a great talker and storyteller, and on looking back over the Records, I find such notes as these: 'Russell attended in great form—abundance of anecdotes'; 'Russell kept us in roars of laughter'; and so on *passim*.

Another great hunting character of the era was old 'Zur Tummus' – Sir Thomas Dyke Acland, 10th Baronet, who died in 1871. He came from a long line of Exmoor squires who started as yeomen farmers in North Devon,

and through the centuries via several advantageous marriages rose to become baronets with vast lands. It was through a particularly fortuitous marriage in 1745 that the Holnicote estate on the eastern edge of Exmoor came into the family, together with the large estate of Pixton near Dulverton. These two areas contain some of the finest hunting country on Exmoor, and the Acland family were not slow to take advantage of this. The great Sir Thomas, as he was popularly known, possibly to distinguish him from his grandfather, father and son, all called Thomas, was a keen supporter of the hunt. He was not, however, quite so enthusiastic as his grandfather, who kept open house after a day's hunting, which would often cover seventy miles, with as many as 500 horsemen in the field.

Along with the estates, the eldest Acland inherited the famous beaver hat, worn in the hunting field and on many other occasions.

ECHOES OF EXMOOR recalled a famous chase when the hat was all but lost. It parted company with its owner while he was chasing the stag in the Barlee valley where, as luck would have it, somehow the hat became impaled upon the quarry's antlers:

the waters of Tarr's Steps, and there he turned at bay. He was taken by the usual lassoo process, with a rope swung over the head—but in this case great care had to be taken not to injure the hat. The ropes were coiled about the slabs that form the bays of this mysterious and pre-historic bridge, and while the stag was thus held tight, the knife was skilfully applied from the bridge behind.

Before the fine beast sunk painlessly into the water, the hat was removed with a resolute twist by the huntsman, and he held it carefully in his hand, amid the silence which generally attends the dispatching of the quarry. Sir Thomas, with only a cap upon his head, viewed the proceedings from his horse in the midst of the multitude, and as every one was gazing and listening, his calm but resonant voice was heard again:

'Will some one please to pass me my hat?'

And here is the story of the end of that hat:

This was the last baronet who wore the beaver hat to which allusion has been made. Beaver-skin hats were the usual top hats during the reign of the Georges, but the silk had now superseded them. Still the Aclands clung lovingly to the traditions of the past even in dress, and what fashion could not do for them in the matter of this hat was at length accomplished by sheer process of decay. This hat had seen ma[n]y 'ups and downs' in the most literal sense. It had been knocked off in the hunting-field, and also at political elections. It had crowned the heads of minors when attaining their majority, and of successive baronets when succeeding to the estates. It had been to the court of no less than four monarchs, and it is said that the jocular Prince of Wales (Edward VII) on hearing of its fame insisted on donning it himself.

In 1867 there was a rent-audit dinner in the George Hotel, South Molton, when for the last time this hat appeared to public view. Sir Thomas was there in person surrounded by his affectionate tenantry with his beaver hat by his side, and when he rose to respond to his toast he held the time honoured head-gear in his hands and after a lengthy speech upon the business of the day he concluded thus: 'Gentleman, there is one little matter of very personal import and of ancestral significance about which the time has come for me to make an announcement, and with that I will conclude. This hat, many of you will remember, I wore when first I met you, and it was worn by my ancestor just one hundred years ago for the first time, and by his successors ever since. It is not from any desire to be more fashionable that I have decided to discard its shape and texture, but on close inspection you will see that it is now incapable of being any longer repaired. I am growing old myself and within a few years at the most, when I am gone, I anticipate that my successor will be unduly agitated between sentiment and the sense of decency, and to save him this pain I now decide to abandon its use.' When he had finished speaking, the worthy farmers hardly knew whether to laugh, to venerate, or to cry, so conflicting were their feelings at this threefold allusion to the hat, the loyalty of his successor, and his own mortality. But at the end, when he said good-bye and insisted on shaking hands with them all, and they saw how feeble and aged he looked, they realized that they had probably seen him for the last time, and then there was

hardly an eye that was not wet with tears as each took a last glance at the old beaver hat.

ECHOES OF EXMOOR, ANON (1925)

Another popular sport on Exmoor was fishing. EXMOOR STREAMS AND ANGLING NOTES was published in 1903, the author, Claude F. Wade, was a barrister at the Temple who visited Exmoor every year. The book contains many fine descriptive passages of the Exmoor streams and waters, of his favourite pools and of angling incidents such as fishermen love to tell each other.

Here he describes his favourite river, the Lyn, followed by a tale that fully illustrates how he combined his legal cunning with his angler's skill to outwit both his prey and his fellow anglers – in the days when fishing was taboo on the Sabbath:

Starting at the beach at Lynmouth through the rough stones of which the Lyn finds its way to the sea, the first object which catches our eyes near low water mark is the salmon weir. This is placed on the right bank of the stream and has existed for a great number of years, though the disused weir between the left bank and the end of the Esplanade is an older one still.

The present weir is rented from the lord of the manor by the proprietors of the Lyndale Hotel and the catches vary a good deal, but there are always salmon and peal waiting in the bay for a flood to take them up stream, and at times very good hauls are made. Perhaps I had better say here that whenever I talk of the right or left bank of a stream, I shall refer to the proper right and left banks, namely, as if we were walking *downwards* with the flow of water, the direction a good trout fisher never walks if he can help it. . . .

We now approach a narrow gorge at the entrance of which stands the celebrated, or I fear perhaps I ought to say notorious, Vellacott's Pool, for its name is more associated with illegal than legal fishing. Get to it on the left bank either by walking all the way up the river on that side, which is a little difficult for old gentlemen, or descend to it by a steep track from the Watersmeet Road. . . .

OLD BRIDGE, NEAR LYNMOUTH

There is a narrow but deep torrent of water, rushing between rocks into the deep spreading pool below, down under the edge of a flat shelf or rock on the left bank. At the head of this gut of tumbling water is the fall, which in a heavy flood gives the salmon pause in his ascent, and the result is that scores of fish, working up through the long wished and waited for spate, lie almost as thick as herrings in a tub below their first check. In this narrow piece of water for many years the salmon were mercilessly 'snatched' or 'stroke-hauled:' a dozen and more rods or rather poles, at first with a single hook with an apology for a worm upon it heavily leaded, then in a more barefaced way with larger hooks, and sometimes even triangles, with heavier lead and with no worm at all, being worked up and down and across. All Lynmouth village, and, alas, some of the visitors, went mad over the 'sport' and a fair amount of money was made out of the sale of the fish, but, thank goodness, after a long period of law-lessness, and certain feeble efforts now and again made by the Taw and Torridge Conservators, the inhabitants themselves came to the rescue and saw that they were killing the goose with the golden eggs,

and that the Lyn was becoming a byword for poaching from which respectable fishermen held aloof. So the thing, at all events in the open and wholesale way stopped, and of late years owing to an excellent combination of the riparian owners, headed by Mr. E.B. Jeune, of Lynmouth Manor House, the river has got back its lost reputation. . . .

In the sixties a well-known actor, who was very fond of salmon fishing in the Lyn, got hold of a monster in the pool under the foot-bridge said to have weighed 40 lb, and I believe nearly died of exhaustion. All day long messengers were going to and from Lynmouth telling the latest stages of the struggle. It was a regular case of 'pull salmon, pull actor,' and as the shades of evening were falling the salmon, helped by the wooden bridge and no doubt the devil, left the actor all alone upon the rocks. How many of us fishermen well know what he felt when that line suddenly went slack, and per-haps we can almost guess some of the words he used. May you, my brother angler, feel happier when you go home from this spot after a good day. . . .

I will tell you a tale of worm fishing in this bit of water, though as far as slimness goes it is rather against myself, and I have been much chaffed about it. On a certain Sunday in the early seventies, during my Oxford days, when Lynmouth was full of keen fishermen and peal were much in request, there was a beautiful and most tempting sight in the stickly pool below the junction of the two rivers in Lynmouth village. Four or five, I forget which, so will take the lesser number, bars of blue were swaying in the stream. They were peal just fresh in from the sea. The fishermen were there all round the bank with their mouths watering; but it being Sunday, the happy fish were absolutely safe from attack, and I think knew it, as they generally seem to do on the great day of rest, and so flaunted themselves before us all throughout the day. But the fishermen thought much each to himself, and each one had some plan how to circumvent the fish and each other on the Monday morning.

I amongst the others secretly kept my council, and the result was this: It would not, of course, be honourable or right to catch them on the Sunday, and so give way to temptation, but I was absolutely determined to be the 'earliest bird,' therefore punctually at one minute past twelve at midnight, I, with a brother-in-law and another soldier friend whom I took into the plot with me, sallied out from our lodging house equipped with my bamboo rod and some strong single gut tackle, a bag of worms, and a dark lantern, and got over the wall by Island Cottage and took up our station on the little beach by the pool. Nobody was about, or if they were, took much notice of us. In went the first worm a yard or two above where I had in the daytime marked the peal—a beautiful bite!—but let him have it for a few seconds,—strike!—and in no time I hauled No. 1 up the beach, and so in less time than an hour I had caught the whole lot, averaging a pound apiece, and went back to bed an excited but contented youth. I woke about 4 a.m. to hear an old friend of mine tramping out in his big boots to forestall other fishermen, little knowing that the peal were all lying bright and beautiful in death in the larder downstairs. I heard afterwards that many others were at that pool, too, and went empty away. For myself I turned over and slept till a late breakfast, a happy but slim fisher.

EXMOOR STREAMS AND ANGLING NOTES, CLAUDE F. WADE (1903)

The riding playground is an apt description of Exmoor, and, Exmoor folk being what they are, it was inevitable that riding in all its forms should at some time make an appearance. Wherever hunting is part of the rural scene, so too will you find the point-to-points. It did not seem popular, however, and, according to this account, only two such events took place:

The Devon and Somerset Staghounds have held two Point to Point Race meetings, and two only; and some interest must attach to these spasmodic efforts to amuse the Exmoor hunting man. Indeed Exmoor, where you can start your field say at Hawkcombe Head and tell them to get to Dunkery Beacon as best they may is an ideal ground for such sport. There it is for all to see, and the man would win whose horse was the best stayer and galloper, while much would depend on the horsemanship of the riders, quite apart from any knowledge of the country.

The first meeting took place Monday 20 September 1897 at Larkbarrow, and aroused great local interest. Unfortunately the course selected being over a very treacherous and almost unfair country, there were two accidents. Mr. J. Yandle's Tiny Tom was killed, and Mr. Morland Greig on Rufus broke his arm. For the Farmers' Race there were eleven entries, and Mr. E. Bawden, now whipper-in to the Devon and Somerset, won it on Reeago by Black and Blue, his father's horse. For the Light Weights' Race there were twenty entries, and Mr. J.C. de Las Casas won it on his horse O.D.V. For the Heavy Weights' Race there were but seven entries, and Mr. J.C. de Las Casas also won this on Mr. C.W. Nelder's Bluestocking. Some years elapsed before the second and last meeting took place, this time over a better course, at Hawkcombe Head.

Perhaps it was the difficulty of finding a suitable site that proved the deterrent. Similar difficulties beset most sports on Exmoor, other than hunting, and these were usually to be found on the outlying flatter areas. Polo, for instance, was played at Porlock:

Polo has of late years made enormous strides in popular favour; and a county so famous as Somerset for its pony blood, and containing so many hunting men, was not likely to be long without a polo club. In 1904 the West Somerset Polo Club became affiliated to the County Polo Association. The season is from 1 April to 15 October. Games or matches are held each Wednesday and Saturday in May and June; on Monday, Wednesday and Saturday in July; and on every non-staghunting day in August, September, October. Early in September the club goes on an invitation tour. The ground at Newbridge near Porlock on the Minehead Road is 260 yds. by 120 yds., and is boarded. Few prettier or more picturesque spots could have been selected than this meadow beside the babbling Horner Brook, under the shade of the wild coppices of Breakneck Gorge, with North Hill and the Selworthy Woods in the near distance.

VICTORIA HISTORY OF SOMERSET (1911)

If polo and point-to-points had difficulty in surviving, how much less likely was it that cricket should even stand a chance! As played on Exmoor it was obviously quite an experience, and according to this account was very different from the civilised matches of lowland areas, played on a pitch that was both smooth and level. This singular pitch in the Valley of Rocks was neither. Cricket is still played under the sentinel tors, but the other pitch referred to, above Glenthorne, has disappeared under the plough:

Minehead has always of late years been strong at cricket, and on a certain morning in August, 1888, we Lynton cricketers trembled when we knew that a break was on its way over eighteen miles of meadow and moorland carrying eleven stalwarts, who we were quite certain were capable of meeting at least double the number of our own men. However, 'they came, they saw, *we* conquered!' When their eleven arrived at the Valley of Rocks, it was quite as we expected and dreaded. Good fellows they were, and good cricketers, including names which have figured in County and Public School teams. I won't mention any of the names on either side, except that the Lynton team was worthily led by the Rev W.E. Cox, our parson. Minehead went in first, and we disposed of them all for six runs! and of this number one player, an Oxford friend of mine, and now a well known master at a large public school, made five. The truth is, they were all utterly helpless against a lob bowler, and looked as if they had never seen this simple kind of bowling in their lives before. I distinctly remember one of the great bats of their side, a stout yeoman farmer, whom I knew well, coming in. He was noted for his scientific batting, and the very first ball he received, which was the regulation slow lob, which pitches in front of the legs and curls on to the middle stump, he most carefully and elegantly played forward to, instead of stepping out and hitting it on the full pitch out of the ground. Of course this ball, much to the batsman's surprise, quietly found its curly way to the same middle stump, its goal; and my friend was so disgusted that he never came near the ground in the afternoon, and refused to go in a second time. Lynton went in and made

a small but quite sufficient score, seventy-nine, and afterwards disposed of Minehead again for thirty-nine, and so won easily in one innings.

It was a 'famous victory.' The lobs got seven wickets for four runs in the first innings, and seven for twenty-one in the second. Two well known cricketing brothers who lived beyond Parracombe and generally played for us helped us much, one bowled excellently all the time at the opposite end and deserved more wickets than he got, and the other made twenty-eight out of the seventy-nine runs scored by Lynton.

We have had many other victories and some defeats, too, on this little Valley of Rocks ground, but the wind has often been a great enemy, and many a time it has been impossible to keep the bails on the wickets. The one failing in our Lynton cricket though, was that we could never get many of the bonâ fide village people to take the game up, but after all there was little wonder in this, for the cricket season came at that time when every villager was naturally making all he could out of the fleeting visitors, and all were so busy over this, that they literally had hardly an hour to spare. Some, however, we did get to help us, chiefly as bowlers, and very useful one's, too. I must say that in June and July when they are not quite so full of work, more efforts might be made to bring out local latent talent. I have also played in some very enjoyable matches high up on the edge of the moor above Glenthorne on the Porlock road. This was real good old country cricket; very few of the players knew much about it, and the umpires absolutely nothing, and as to the ground—well the happiest and most comforting period in the day was when your two innings were over and you found yourself still a living man, especially when a very fast bowler in the Cambridge eleven had been pegging away all he knew at your shrinking form.

EXMOOR STREAMS AND ANGLING NOTES, CLAUDE F. WADE (1903)

There was even a golf course at Caffyns, above Lynton. This has long fallen into disrepair and is once again occupied by grazing sheep (there is a plan afoot to resurrect it):

EXFORD, FROM THE RECREATION FIELD

And Matta sleeps there now, I think, in his lonely mound on the height in full view of his unknown brother chief of Trentishoe Barrow.

Or was his tumulus cut into in the early nineties to make the little nine hole course which then came into existence? For links there were on the top of this moor and not such bad ones either, the greens being quite good. Stones formed the drawback, and if one got off the fairway, good-bye to your ball in the gorse and heather. The pro., I remember, had a clever little terrier who would retrieve out of the thickest roughty-toughty, and on a crowded links would have been a source of much profit to his master. But no one ever played here except ourselves, and the rare labourer who passed would eye our efforts in amaze and thus unburden his soul at night:

'Hev'e zeen thiccy lil ole geame of jolf, Gaarge?'

'Noa, what like be 'un?'

'There be two as plays 'un, and one of 'un makes a lil heap of muck an' putts a lil ball up over, and then her hits 'un—her hits 'un as hard as ever her can. An' then they goes an' looks vor 'un. An' they looks an' they looks for most a half hour an' at last they vinds 'un. An' when hers vound 'un, whoy danged if her doan't hit 'un again!'

It was a little known game in those parts then and not so long established in England. Indeed, I remember playing at Westward Ho! in 1880 when that course and Blackheath were the only two South of Tweed.

Well, the links are gone now; the sheep have demolished the bunkers and the greens have vanished under the all-conquering heather. Aesthetically the change is for the better. The little wooden pavilion stood on the road overlooking the sea towards Wales; the first two holes ran South and then crossed the road East, about half a mile from which point the Lynton links on Caffyns Down were situated. Thence the line returned to Martinhoe Cross where stood the fifth green closely guarded by two roads. One short hole to the West and then a straight long three to the home green.

Here I met once with a curious adventure. Teeing off from the fourth green I struck what was probably the finest drive I ever did in my life—a screamer, of low trajectory and heading for the pin. Visions of a hole in one crossed my mind. A hole it was, but of another kind, for to my horror at that identical moment over the brow of the road came a carriage and pair. In vain I invoked the High Gods. Straight into that carriage panel went that ball; the carriage stopped; there was a pause; the door flew open and out bundled an old gentleman, purple in the face, and advanced towards me. There was no covert so I had to face the music. Judge of my surprise when instead of the winged words I was expecting he offered profuse apologies for spoiling what he was good enough to term my magnificent drive! Sporting old boy! I made his better acquaintance afterwards.

It was pleasant up there even when things went adversely for one's ball. You must remember that in those days the amenities of the place were unspoiled; no little railway in the offing to disfigure the moor, no telegraph poles, no new roads to bring the traffic, but a glorious view of the sea and coast line with Wales occasionally visible in the far distance, though from the point of view of fine weather this was considered very undesirable.

HOUNDS MEET AT DUNSTER

Games do not appeal to the native, partly from lack of numbers, opportunity, and level ground. The only one which flourished then (but which I hear nothing of now) was throwing the hammer. This was the regulation sixteen-pound weight mounted on a long haft, and was swung to and fro, underhand, until sufficient momentum was attained. A friend and I—he was a burly Yorkshireman and should have played cricket for his 'Varsity—used to compete every morning with varying success until our hands got too sore, but we were generally beaten about six inches by the postman, who was the local champion, and would always stop on his rounds to have a throw. Time is of no account in these parts.

A few pages back I spoke of ring-goal. This is a game which has completely gone out and for which you cannot now buy the implements. An improved variant of the older La Grace, it was played by two, each armed with two ash sticks about three feet long and tapering to a point, and a leather-covered cane ring about the size of a soup-plate. You stood about fifty yards apart and hurled the ring off the sticks, one being held stationary while the other supplied the propulsion. The second player had to catch it on the point of his sticks. When properly thrown the ring would fly very fast straight at you in a horizontal plane, so that a catch was by no means easy, and if you missed it, broken teeth might follow. Originally there were two goals behind the players, which accounts for the name, but these soon disappeared. It was a good game and deserved popularity.

EXMOOR, W. SHERRACOMBE (1920)

TWELVE

Country Talk

Summer visitors who only see the benign face of the moor, with the sun shining on Dunkery and the waters of the Bristol Channel a sparkling blue in the background, might benefit from a glimpse of Exmoor in winter. The wide, open uplands are very different when the heather is dead, and the bracken brown and withered:

November
This is the forlorn time of the year's decay, of wind and rain beating the last leaves from the empty branches of trees; the time of blurred window panes, of emptying interest in the country, of summer joys of the old village remembered with regret.

From the upper western room of the cottage I saw the forest trees swaying in the mighty orchestration of the south-west gale, which brought the grey Atlantic rain to the unfamiliar valley. Day after day the rain had been blowing up the valley, night after night the wind had mumbled across the wide square chimneys. Every hopeful gleam in the clouds was dulled by the hiss and splash on the window panes, while the fiercer gusts blew bubbles of water under the casements. Day after day, staring at the flawed panes—then suddenly the spaniel, who had done nothing but sleep with feet and nose in the embers of the wood fire, was leaping and barking, for he heard the rattle of the ash plant being taken from the stand by the door. Let rain soak, blow wind, forget the past, this life is most jolly; let the alleged bogs of Exmoor engulf if they can. Shall it be the Sportsman's Inn? Pull the door back against the blustering rain. Dog and man shall fight the wind to-day.

It was good to feel warm strength in the hollow roar of the trees, to stride the long way to the high ground of the bleak moors among the faded mummified bells of the heather, where from the tufts of the cotton grass the snipe arose in small, sharp, crooked flight before the dog. The world, with the petty cares of one's own making, lay below, fields and hedges, valleys and hillocks, hundreds and thousands of multi-shapen patches diminishing and losing colour until the remote country merged and was lost in ocean vapour. Dog and I were alone with the water-plashes and the frantic wind-music of the moor. Twenty miles distant a sun-shaft, piercing the discoloration of the storm, lit many fields, travelling fast yet seeming not to move, small as a bright spot on a butterfly's wing. So we travelled, hour after hour.

The last farm, dim-seen within bent beeches, was left behind. Here wild ponies stood long-tailed and wet, in the lee of a ragged beech-hedge; and among the bog-plashes, shadowy and slim creatures fled away into the mist. What had brought the red deer into the open? Usually they lie 'under the wind' among the trees of the coombes, or valleys.

Then at last we were on the Forest of Exmoor, the treeless, yellow, ancient moor. The rain could soak no more. Its sting glowed on the cheek. The dog trotted to heel, tired after his vain search for rabbits. He had run thrice the journey I had made.

A wild twilight took the last of autumn's colours from the day. Home, which was a weary place after the days spent, or wasted, indoors, now glowed.

'COUNTRY OF THE RAIN', HENRY WILLIAMSON (1930)

J.B.H. Peel was a well-known writer on country matters who contributed regularly to the Daily Telegraph. *Several of his articles appeared in book form:*

COUNTRY TALK and COUNTRY TALK AGAIN. Peel was a great admirer of Exmoor, retiring to a cottage in the Heddon Valley below Parracombe. He is commemorated by a plaque in the car-park at County Gate. His descriptions of the sometimes severe climatic conditions experienced by those who live on the moor are vivid. Here is Exmoor in her winter guise:

Blizzard

At dawn the wind abated, but not the cold. At noon the clouds formed a single sheet, grey and very low. At three o'clock, in premature darkness, snow seemed imminent. Ten minutes later it arrived, flouncing like feathers from a sky so still that the flakes fell in straight lines, covering all things equally. Even while you watched, tussocks of grass turned white. At one moment the world was apparently unpeopled; at the next, life bustled in every cottage and farm. Housewives appeared, snatching linen from the clothes line, cradling logs in the porch, dragging perambulators to the shed. Firelit windows reflected John Clare's wintry scene:

> While snows the window panes bedim
> The fire curls up a sunny charm
> Where creaming o'er the pitcher's rim
> The flowering ale is set to warm.

Children stared up at the sky, and one of them held out the palm of her hand, as though the flakes were manna from heaven. Footsteps changed from a clop to a crunch, sounding the same on gravel as on grass. An infinite universe contracted into a claustrophobic continuum which excluded both the sky and the skyline, substituting instead a damp and whitewashed wall.

At four o'clock a car's headlights shone from the moor, then halted and went back, the motorist having decided that reversal was the better part of discretion, for snow would soon obliterate the landmarks. All sounds were muffled, and some scarcely audible. But keen ears could detect the snow as it struck the leaves of a holly bush with repeated soft blows that created a rustle. At six o'clock the hayricks wore a white thatch, nearly as tall as a chef's cap. Then a breeze stirred, and became a wind and finally a gale which, instead of scattering the clouds, called-up reinforcements, hurling the blizzard against walls, windows, and whatever else stood in its way. There were no dainty snowflakes now, no graceful curtsies. The charming ballet had become a menacing reality, stinging the eye, sealing the lashes, thrusting a cold hand through collars and cuffs.

In mountainous country the natives are accustomed to snow. When it does arrive they take certain precautions, often by telephone. 'Gran?' says a voice. 'It's Florrie speaking. Is Dad still there? Well, just tell 'en to get cracking. Why? The snow, of course. Lord bless us, midear, don't 'ee never look out o' the window?' Some people allow a neighbour to pave the way. 'Idris here. Cwm Fawr. You'll soon be having a tractor coming up, I shouldn't wonder. You will? In that case, I'll risk taking the car.' At remote crofts in the Scottish Highlands, where the snowscape may be several weeks old, even the rent collector comes as a pleasant surprise. 'Why, it's Fergus Macmoneybags. Sit ye doon, mon. We've no' seen a soul since Thairsday.'

The snow is drifting now, blocking lanes at an angle of forty-five degrees. Signposts on the high moor sink from sight while cattle wander in search of shelter, and the red deer re-enact Edward Thomas's nightpiece:

> Out in the dark over the snow
> The fallow fawn invisible go
> With the fallow doe;
> And the winds blow
> Fast as the stars are slow.

Meanwhile, unheard above the gale, three telephone wires snap, leaving their strands to sway like frisky pendula. As though mimicking a jingle-bell sleigh ride, the postman's van clinks its chains, for the Royal Mail comes and goes regardless of the weather. Twice

PLOUGHING NEAR WATCHET

already the postman has lent his shovel to a motorist whose rear wheels skidded into a drift. Suddenly the gloom is gashed by vivid gleams from a snowplough worming its way uphill. 'Just my luck,' the driver tells his mate. 'Bingo night and a bloody blizzard.' He points to a cottage at the far end of a blocked track. 'While we'm yere we may as well give access to Grannie Newton. The poor soul's been on her own since Tom died.' The driver makes a brief detour. A door opens, shuts, re-opens after five minutes, and back churns the plough. 'Game old girl is Grannie. Ah, and her makes a good cup o' tea, too. If only . . . 'old 'ard, mate! Another wire down.' The driver peers ahead. 'And yere's some madman taking a midnight stroll.'

Waist-high in drifts, an oilskinned youth looms out of the whiteness.

'Are you lost,' shouts the driver, 'or just loony?'

'Neither,' comes the reply. 'I'm on my way to see how Mrs Newton's doing.'

'Her's doing fine. Radio full-blast, a fire halfway up the chimney, tea all round, and a bottle o' ginger wine to keep the witches away. But 'twas a kindly thought, all the same.' He quizzes the sou'-westered face. 'Are you Joe Davey's boy?'

'That's me.'

'I thought as much. I can recognise a Davey nose afore ever it opens its mouth. Hop on board, and we'll take 'ee as far as the crossroads.' The plough lurches forward again. 'Old Joe's soon going to have to do some digging.'

'We'm digging already,' the youth replies. 'Some o' the ewes was six foot deep. And the ponies don't like it neither. Still, we'm used to it up yere.'

Already the snow has thinned the tyremarks, and a wind carries away the voices. Soon the red lamps disappear in a white void. No one is out of doors who can sit beside the fire. But the birds and certain other wild creatures are less fortunate. Although feather and fur may protect them against the cold, only chance or a compassionate cottager will supply their breakfast.

COUNTRY TALK AGAIN, J.H.B. PEEL (1970)

Although the story is good in itself, it is the descriptive passages that assure LORNA DOONE *a place in the heart of all Exmoor lovers. Here is Blackmore's description of a hard winter on the moor:*

Through that season of bitter frost, the red deer of the forest, having nothing to feed upon, and no shelter to rest in, had grown accustomed to our ricks of corn, and hay, and clover. There we might see a hundred of them, almost any morning, come for warmth, and food, and comfort, and scarce willing to move away. And many of them were so tame, that they quietly presented themselves at our back door, and stood there with their coats quite stiff, and their flanks drawn in and panting, and icicles sometimes on their chins, and their great eyes fastened wistfully upon any merciful person; craving for a bit of food, and a drink of water. I suppose that they had not sense enough to chew the snow and melt it; at any rate, all the springs being frozen, and rivers hidden out of sight, these poor things suffered even more from thirst than they did from hunger.

But now there was no fear of thirst, and more chance indeed of drowning; for a heavy gale of wind arose, with violent rain from the south-west, which lasted almost without a pause, for three nights and two days. At first, the rain made no impression on the bulk of snow, but ran from every sloping surface, and froze on every flat one, through the coldness of the earth; and so it became impossible for any man to keep his legs, without the help of a shodden staff. After a good while, however, the air growing very much warmer, this state of things began to change, and a worse one to succeed it; for now the snow came thundering down from the roof, and rock, and ivied tree, and floods began to roar and foam in every trough and gulley. The drifts that had been so white and fair, looked yellow, and smirched, and muddy, and lost their graceful curves, and moulded lines and airyness. But the strangest sight of all to me was in the bed of streams, and brooks, and especially of the Lynn river. It was worth going miles to behold such a thing, for a man might never have the chance again.

Vast drifts of snow had filled the valley, and piled above the river-course, fifty feet high in many places, and in some as much as a hundred. These had frozen over the top, and glanced the rain away from them, and being sustained by rock, and tree, spanned the water mightily. But meanwhile the waxing flood, swollen from every moorland hollow, and from every spouting crag, had dashed away all icy fetters, and was rolling gloriously. Under white fantastic arches, and long tunnels freaked and fretted, and between pellucid pillars jagged with nodding architraves, the red impetuous torrent rushed, and the brown foam whirled and flashed. I was half inclined to jump in, and swim through such glorious scenery; for nothing used to please me more than swimming in a flooded river. But I thought of the rocks, and I thought of the cramp, and more than all, of Lorna; and so, between one thing and another, I let it roll on without me.

LORNA DOONE, R.D. BLACKMORE (1869)

A landscape without people is empty indeed, and Exmoor deserted by its natives would be nothing more than a showplace.

Here, from J.H.B. Peel again, is a delightful account of harvest-time, and a farmer's view that God didn't rightly understand the needs of farmers – but then, He's a 'foreigner' too!:

'The corn was orient and immortal wheat, which never should be reaped, nor was ever sown. I thought it had stood from everlasting to everlasting.' This corn, however, was not immortal, for the harvesters were already climbing the hill; nor had the corn stood *ab initio*, for I had watched the ploughing of its seedbed and the harrowing of its tilth. How distant those dark days seemed; how remote the rain and the mist and the teatime lamplight. Even the later days were dim . . . those cuckoo-dawns in April, those rosebud sunsets in May. And now, once again, another year had waned. . . .

My thoughts went back to another parched summer and to the farmer who tempered his *Confitebor tibi* with a respectful admonition: 'I marvel we'm reaping at all. The soil is like pepper. 'T'wasn't all that while ago I said, "We'll not need a reaper this year. What we'll need is a plough, and then start all over again." But there it is. God

always sends us something in the end. I do truly wish, though, He wouldn't wrap His blessings in such zany weather. 'Tis as though He'd no knowledge of farming. No knowledge at all. That's what I find so puzzling. But there it is. I'll just about cover my costs. Leastways I won't have to pay no income tax to subsidise somebody's strike picket.'

The three harvesters were in sight now, shirt-sleeved and thirsty as they halted to swig cider from a whisky bottle. The farmer and the tractor driver, being elderly, wore shirts, but the youngster was stripped to his waist. As they drew near I overheard the veterans discussing a bygone harvest. 'Must ha' been 1921 since we suffered such a teetotal September. I remember it well. Not a sign o' rain from Rogation to Michaelmas. And when at last the corn really was ripe, blow me down if the rain didn't start, and th'old farmer . . . a reg'lar Methody . . . he yelled out, "Strong drink is a mocker. You'm not touching a drop o' my cider till the last stook is gathered." And by golly we didn't. But th'old fella made up for it when he give us an 'arvest supper. "Men," he said, "don't never breathe a word o' this to the elders o' the chapel, but in those two casks," he said, "there's enough cider to get 'ee pissed for a twelvemonth." Reuben he was called. Reuben Buckland. Lived to be ninety did old Reub. And his last words were, "Call me five o'clock tomorrow morning." So they did. But he never answered 'cause he'd risen earlier than expected.'

Then the reaper went into action, and the blades whirled, and the corn fell, and the sun shone, and the men stooked. And when they had gone home to supper, the moon came up, vast as a cosmic orange; and a rabbit crinkled through the stubble, and an owl hooted from the coppice, and the good earth slept among the sheaves.

COUNTRY TALK AGAIN, J.H.B. PEEL (1970)

The friendly, helpful nature of the moorfolk impressed itself on Richard Jefferies, who spent much time with the farmers and huntsmen while writing his book RED DEER. He describes a farming fraternity very much dependent on self-help for oneself, and between neighbours:

THRESHING AT WITHYCOMBE

Something else, too, besides the red deer has survived, and that is courtesy. Go wherever you will in red deer country you will be met with politeness, hospitality, and readiness to oblige. If you are thirsty, you have only to knock at the nearest door, and, according to your taste, you can partake of cider or milk; and it is ten to one you are asked to enter and spend half an hour in a pleasant gossip. Everywhere there is welcome, and the slightest incident is sufficient introduction; everywhere hospitality, and everywhere politeness. On the road every man you meet, according to his station, nods his head or touches his hat, and no one passes another without saluting. Walk down the village street, and all who are about, in their gardens, at their doors, on horseback or afoot, wish you 'Good morning.' This is not only observed towards visitors, but amongst themselves.

Farmers salute farmers; labourers and employers acknowledge each other's presence. The difference is so marked between these habits of personal courtesy, and those that prevail in large towns, that it seems like another country altogether. Nor is it a superficial courtesy, but backed by a real willingness to oblige. Any one with an interest in sport, antiquities, old china, old furniture, finds not the least difficulty in his way, but can satisfy his curiosity to the full.

As an instance of the real goodwill that subsists under the outward politeness may be mentioned the bees at sheep-shearing time. The farmers and farmers' sons at that season visit each farm in succession—twenty, thirty, or more of them together sit down in the barn and shear the sheep. It is a regular bee, on the American pattern, or rather the adventurers from Westward Ho! carried the custom with them across the Atlantic. A farmer who would not assist his neighbour at such a time and join the party would be regarded as a churl; but, as a matter of fact, none ever do refuse.

RED DEER, RICHARD JEFFERIES (1884)

Harvest home is not the only lost custom, although it is encouraging that, latterly, some of the old skills and traditions are being revived, and, of course, some survive in the annual carnivals still held in the larger villages and towns. Here are a handful recalling 'the neck' of harvest-time, and the primeval custom of wassailing the apple tree:

Old customs are rapidly passing out of mind here as elsewhere. One may be said to be quite dead, though not yet out of mind. The reaping machine has killed the 'neck' or 'knack.' The 'neck' was a kind of figure made of a small quantity of the ears of the last corn reaped, twisted or tied together. Brand, describing the custom as it was observed in Devon in his day, says, 'When they have cut the corn the reapers assemble together, a knack is made which one placed in the middle of the company holds up, crying thrice 'a knack,' which all the rest repeat: the person in the middle then says

Well cut! well bound!
Well shocked! well saved from the ground!

He afterwards cries 'whoop,' and his companions hollow as loud as they can. So far his description tallies pretty well with our local practice, but there was more that was exciting to follow. The next move was to get the neck into the farmer's house without discovery. The women laid wait for the men with vessels of water. If the bearer of the image was so unfortunate as to expose it to a wetting he was in bad strait, for he had but little cider. The sacred thing was therefore carefully concealed, and many a man was drenched from a window, being an object of suspicion, before the neck got into the house. Once in, it was hung up to remain until superseded by its successor of the following harvest. There is much speculation as to the origin of this custom and its early significance. That it was followed in very early times in the district is plain. The rolls of the bailiff of Porlock refer to an annual expenditure for 'the custom called le necke.' In the second roll 14*d*. was the sum paid for victuals for the tenants and household in observance of the custom. This is the earliest recorded instance known to me.

Another popular custom is not quite dead. It is not observed as it was, but probably some vitality may be left in it so long as orchard owners are prepared to find a few pecks of cider for a Twelfth-night ceremony. To 'wassail' the apple-trees was considered an obligation if a good crop, and therefore much cider, was to be expected. When the neighbours were assembled in the orchard a large bowl of hot cider, with toast therein, was put into the fork of an apple tree, and everyone who could helped himself with a spoon, one dip each and no more. Naturally this was not the only cider that was drunk. As a rule the party was prepared to dispose of as much as the owner of the orchard cared to provide. Portions of the toast, or bread, were hung upon the trees for the birds. A song was sung with a shouting chorus, emphasized by the discharge of guns. Here it is, as it was taken down by me from one who has often sung it:

> Old apple tree, I wassail thee,
> And hope that thou wilt bear,
> For the Lord doth know where we shall be
> To be merry another year;
> To blow well and to bear well,
> And so merry let us be.
> Let every man drink off his cup;
> Here's health to the Old Apple Tree.

Shouting Chorus.

> Old apple tree, I wassail thee,
> And hope that thou wilt bear
> Hats full, caps full,
> Three bushel bags full,
> Tallat holes full,
> Little heap under the stairs.
> Hip, hip, hip, hurrah! hurrah!
> Guns – Bang, bang, bang!

Here came pitchers of cider, and so the fun went on , only measured by the host's hospitality. The night of the 17th January, old Twelfth Day, was the wassailing night of the district.

WINSFORD

Folk still run for a little space when they hear the cuckoo for the first time in the spring, lest they should pass an idle year. Now and then a bride is 'chained' at the church gate or elsewhere on her path from church. A chain, or, for want of it, a rope, adorned with flowers, is held across her way. If the bridegroom be a shoemaker he may see a pair of old shoes among the flowers; if a currier, a sheep's horn, and so on according to his trade. Whoever he may be, the chain will not be lowered until he lighten his pocket, and it is poor compliment to keep the bride waiting. I have heard of flowers held before the face of a bride in the church porch 'for luck,' and one old woman was well known for the skill she displayed in securing the best place for the ceremony at every wedding.

VICTORIA HISTORY OF SOMERSET (1911)

Minehead's famous hobby-horse may have been waning in popularity when this account was written, but happily it has survived, and today still prances round the streets on May Day. It is doubtful whether today's children would find anything in the old hobby-horse to terrify them!:

HAYRICKS AT HARVEST TIME

Minehead is the headquarters of a curious custom, known as 'hobby-horsing.' Until recently it was indulged in with much vigour, and is even now, apparently, very far from moribund. On May Day a number of men and boys, accompanied by a drum, perambulated the streets, grotesquely attired, and surrounding the figure of the hobby-horse—a rude imitation of the quadruped, formed by two men concealed beneath trappings, with an imitation of a horse's head attached, and, not unfrequently, a formidable hempen tail as well, wherewith the unwary, as well as those refusing to pay a small fee to the revellers, were lightly beaten. So much for my own recollection. Other items of the performance which were formerly carried out consisted of 'booting' or 'pursing,' *i.e.*, rapping the recalcitrant with a boot. At Dunster Castle the party was treated to refreshments and rewarded for their performances with money. A recent writer on the customs of this part of the world says that the festivities commenced by the inhabitants dancing round the hobby-horse at the cross-roads outside the town in the direction of Bidcombe, and terminated on May 3rd at other cross-roads on the highway to Porlock.

The origin of the hobby-horse has never, perhaps, been quite satisfactorily explained. Of one thing, however, there can, I think, be no doubt, viz., that it is a relic of the old morris-dance:

> The hobby-horse doth hither prance,
> Maid Marian and the Morris-Dance;

and Tollet imagines that it represents 'the King of the May,' while another fancies that it commemorates 'a religious fracas, long ago, in which one party trounced the other.' Savage opines that here it is the relic of some ancient custom of beating the bounds. Whatever it may perpetuate, it was, and is, to adults of the lower classes, an interesting ceremony, though to young children the appalling form of the steed, and the alarming appearance of his satellites, are fraught with some terror.

EXMOOR, J.L.W. PAGE (1890)

THIRTEEN

Dear Lorna

Romance and wild scenery go hand in hand, and areas of unspoilt beauty have always proved an attraction to the artistic instincts. Exmoor has proved popular with artists of all kinds, though most have preferred to portray the kinder scenery of the valleys and the picturesque villages around the periphery. It takes a bold brush to master the wide landscapes of the open moor.

Many writers, too, have visited Exmoor and have given us widely varying narratives, but LORNA DOONE has done more for Exmoor than any other. The author, Richard Blackmore, spent much of his childhood on and around Exmoor. It was his playground and he explored it freely, and his love and knowledge of the country was deep and intimate. The novel was first published in 1869 and, as with Blackmore's earlier works, seemed doomed to sink into oblivion. One of those strange quirks of fortune rescued it – Queen Victoria's granddaughter married a Scottish peer, which on the face of it seems hardly likely to improve the sales of a book dealing with Exmoor. But the Doones were said by some to be outlawed Scottish nobility, and just as Lorna was marrying beneath her by accepting John Ridd, so was the Princess Louise by marrying a man not of royal blood. The final push was given by an account that appeared, erroneously comparing the story to the family history of the bridegroom, the Marquis of Lorne. From then on, dear Lorna has never looked back.

In his preface to the sixth edition, Blackmore wrote:

Few things have surprised me more, and nothing has more pleased me, than the great success of this simple tale. For truly it is a grand success, to win the attention and kind regard not of the general public only, but also of those who are at home with the scenery, people, life and language, wherein a native cannot always satisfy the natives.

Therefore, any son of Devon may imagine, and will not grudge, the writer's delight at hearing from a recent visitor to the west that 'Lorna Doone' to a Devonshire man, is as good as clotted cream, almost!' Although not half as good as that, it has entered many a tranquil happy pure and hospitable home: and the author, while deeply grateful for this genial reception ascribes it partly to the fact that his story contains no word, or thought, disloyal to its birthright in the fairest county of England.

The passage that has caused most problems to those who cannot rest until they have related fiction to fact is the description of the famous, or infamous, water slide. Of course it is exaggerated, but LORNA DOONE is a work of the imagination, not a guide book. Here is the passage itself, beginning with Jan's lovely description of catching loach, which was the reason for the expedition in the first place:

But when I was turned fourteen years old, and put into good small-clothes, buckled at the knees, and strong blue worsted hosen, knitted by my mother, it happened to me without choice, I may say, to explore the Bagworthy water. And it came about in this wise.

My mother had long been ailing, and not well able to eat much; and there is nothing that frightens us so much as for people to have no love of their victuals. Now I chanced to remember, that once at the time of the holidays, I had brought dear mother from Tiverton a jar of pickled loaches, caught by myself in the Lowman river, and baked in the kitchen oven, with vinegar, a few leaves of bay, and about a dozen peppercorns. And mother had said that, in all her life,

BADGWORTHY WATER AND DOONE VALLEY

she had never tasted anything fit to be compared with them. Whether she said so good a thing, out of compliment to my skill in catching the fish and cooking them, or whether she really meant it, is more than I can tell, though I quite believe the latter, and so would most people who tasted them; at any rate, I now resolved to get some loaches for her, and do them in the self-same manner, just to make her eat a bit. . . .

But let me be of any age, I never could forget that day, and how bitter cold the water was. For I doffed my shoes and hose, and put them into a bag about my neck; and left my little coat at home, and tied my shirt-sleeves back to my shoulders. Then I took a three-pronged fork firmly bound to a rod with cord, and a piece of canvas kerchief, with a lump of bread inside it; and so went into the pebbly water, trying to think how warm it was. . . .

A long way down that limpid water, chill and bright as an iceberg, went my little self that day, on man's choice errand—destruction. All the young fish seemed to know that I was one who had taken out God's certificate, and meant to have the value of it; every one of them was aware, that we desolate more than replenish the earth. For a cow might come and look into the water, and put her yellow lips down; a kingfisher, like a blue arrow, might shoot through the dark alleys over the channel, or sit on a dipping withy-bough, with his beak sunk into his breast-feathers; even an otter might float downstream, likening himself to a log of wood, with his flat head flush with the water top, and his oily eyes peering quietly; and yet no panic would seize other life, as it does when a sample of man comes.

Now let not any one suppose that I thought of these things when I was young, for I knew not the way to do it. And proud enough in truth I was, at the universal fear I spread in all those lonely places, where I myself must have been afraid, if anything had come up at me. It is all very pretty to see the trees, big with their hopes of another year, though dumb as yet on the subject, and the waters murmuring gaiety, and the banks spread out with comfort; but a boy takes none of this to heart, unless he be meant for a poet (which no man ever can charge on me), and he would liefer have a good apple, or even a bad one, if he stole it.

When I had travelled two miles or so, conquered now and then with cold, and coming out to rub my legs into a lively friction, and only fishing here and there because of the tumbling water; suddenly, in an open space, where meadows spread about it, I found a good stream flowing softly into the body of our brook. And it brought, so far as I could guess by the sweep of it under my knee-caps, a larger power of clear water than the Lynn itself had; only it came more quietly down, not being troubled with stairs and steps, as the fortune of the Lynn is, but gliding smoothly and forcibly, as if upon some set purpose.

Hereupon I drew up, and thought, and reason was much inside me; because the water was bitter cold, and my little toes were aching. So on the bank I rubbed them well with a sprout of young sting-nettle, and having skipped about awhile, was kindly inclined to eat a bit.

Now all the turn of all my life hung upon that moment. But as I sat there munching a crust of Betty Muxworthy's sweet brown bread, and a bit of cold bacon along with it, and kicking my little red heels against the dry loam to keep them warm. I knew no more than fish under the fork, what was going on over me. It seemed a sad business to go back now, and tell Annie there were no loaches; and yet it was a frightful thing, knowing what I did of it, to venture, where no grown man durst, up the Bagworthy water. And please to recollect that I was only a boy in those days, fond enough of anything new, but not like a man to meet it.

However, as I ate more and more, my spirit arose within me, and I thought of what my father had been, and how he had told me a hundred times, never to be a coward. And then I grew warm, and my little heart was ashamed of its pit-a-patting, and I said to myself, 'now if father looks, he shall see that I obey him.' So I put the bag round my neck again, and buckled my breeches far up from the knee, expecting deeper water, and crossing the Lynn, went stoutly up under the branches which hang so dark on the Bagworthy river.

I found it strongly over-woven, turned, and torn with thicket-wood, but not so rocky as the Lynn, and more inclined to go evenly. There were bars of chafed stakes stretched from the sides halfway across the current, and light outriders of pithy weed, and blades of last year's water-grass trembling in the quiet places, like a spider's threads, on the transparent stillness, with a tint of olive moving it; and here and there the sun came in, as if his light were sifted, making dance upon the waves, and shadowing the pebbles.

Here, although affrighted often by the deep, dark places, and feeling that every step I took might never be taken backward, on the whole I had very comely sport of loaches, trout, and minnows, forking some, and tickling some, and driving others to shallow nooks, whence I could bail them ashore. Now, if you have ever been fishing, you will not wonder that I was led on, forgetting all about danger, and taking no heed of the time, but shouting in a childish way, whenever I caught a 'whacker' (as we called a big fish at Tiverton); and in sooth there were very fine loaches here, having more lie and harbourage than in the rough Lynn stream, though not quite so large as in the Lowman, where I have even taken them to the weight of a quarter of a pound.

But in answer to all my shouts, there never was any sound at all, except of a rocky echo, or a scared bird hustling away, or the sudden dive of a water-vole; and the place grew thicker and thicker, and the covert grew darker above me, until I thought that the fishes might have good chance of eating me, instead of my eating the fishes.

For now the day was falling fast behind the brown of the hill-tops; and the trees, being void of leaf and hard, seemed giants ready to beat me. And every moment, as the sky was clearing up for a white frost, the cold of the water got worse and worse, until I was fit to cry with it. And so, in a sorry plight, I came to an opening in the bushes, where a great black pool lay in front of me, whitened with snow (as I thought) at the sides, till I saw it was only foam-froth.

Now, though I could swim with great ease and comfort, and feared no depth of water, when I could fairly come to it, yet I had no desire to go over head and ears into this great pool, being so cramped and weary, and cold enough in all conscience, though wet only up to the middle, not counting my arms and shoulders. And the look of this black pit was enough to stop one from diving into it,

even on a hot summer's day with sunshine on the water; I mean, if the sun ever shone there. As it was, I shuddered and drew back; not alone at the pool itself, and the black air there was about it, but also at the whirling manner, and wisping of white threads upon it, in stripy circles round and round; and the centre still as jet.

But soon I saw the reason of the stir and depth of that great pit, as well as of the roaring sound which long had made me wonder. For skirting round one side, with very little comfort, because the rocks were high and steep, and the ledge at the foot so narrow, I came to a sudden sight and marvel, such as I never dreamed of. For, lo! I stood at the foot of a long pale slide of water, coming smoothly to me, without any break or hindrance, for a hundred yards or more, and fenced on either side with cliff, sheer, and straight, and shining. The water neither ran nor fell, nor leaped with any spouting, but made one even slope of it, as if it had been combed or planed, and looking like a plank of deal laid down a deep black staircase. However there was no side-rail, nor any place to walk upon, only the channel a fathom wide, and the perpendicular walls of crag shutting out the evening.

The look of this place had a sad effect, scaring me very greatly, and making me feel that I would give something, only to be at home again, with Annie cooking my supper, and our dog, 'Watch,' sniffing upward. But nothing would come of wishing; that I had long found out; and it only made one the less inclined to work without white feather. So I laid the case before me in a little council; not for loss of time, but only that I wanted rest, and to see things truly.

Then says I to myself, – 'John Ridd, these trees, and pools, and lonesome rocks, and setting of the sunlight, are making a gruesome coward of thee. Shall I go back to my mother so, and be called her fearless boy?'

Nevertheless, I am free to own that it was not any fine sense of shame which settled my decision; for indeed there was nearly as much of danger in going back as in going on, and perhaps even more of labour, the journey being so roundabout. But that which saved me from turning back was a strange inquisitive desire, very unbecoming in a boy of little years; in a word, I would risk a great deal to know, what made the water come down like that, and what there was at the top of it.

Therefore, seeing hard strife before me, I girt up my breeches anew, with each buckle one hole tighter, for the sodden straps were stretching and giving, and mayhap my legs were grown smaller from the coldness of it. Then I bestowed my fish around my neck more tightly, and not stopping to look much, for fear of fear, crawled along over the fork of rocks, where the water had scooped the stone out; and shunning thus the ledge from whence it rose, like the mane of a white horse, into the broad black pool, softly I let my feet into the dip and rush of the torrent.

And here I had reckoned without my host, although (as I thought) so clever; and it was much but that I went down into the great black pool, and had never been heard of more; and this must have been the end of me, except for my trusty loachfork. For the green wave came down, like great bottles upon me, and my legs were gone off in a moment, and I had not time to cry out with wonder, only to think of my mother and Annie, and knock my head very sadly, which made it go round so that brains were no good, even if I had any. But all in a moment, before I knew aught, except that I must die out of the way, with a roar of water upon me, my fork, praise God, stuck fast in the rock, and I was borne up upon it. I felt nothing, except that here was another matter to begin upon; and it might be worth while, or again it might not, to have another fight for it. But presently the dash of the water upon my face revived me, and my mind grew used to the roar of it; and meseemed I had been worse off than this, when first flung into the Lowman.

Therefore I gathered my legs back slowly, as if they were fish to be landed, stopping whenever the water flew too strongly off my shin-bones, and coming along, without sticking out to let the wave get hold of me. And in this manner I won a footing, leaning well forward like a draught-horse, and balancing on my strength as it were, with the ashen stake set behind me. Then I said to myself, 'John Ridd, the sooner you get yourself out by the way you came, the bet-ter it will be for you.' But to my great dismay and affright, I saw that no choice was left me now, except that I must climb somehow up that hill of water, or else be washed down into the pool, and whirl around till it drowned me. For there was no chance of fetching back, by the way I had gone down into it; and further up was a hedge of rock on either side of the water-way, rising a hundred yards in height, and for all I could tell five hundred, and no place to set a foot in.

Having said the Lord's Prayer (which was all I knew), and made a very bad job of it, I grasped the good loach-stick under a knot, and steadied me with my left hand, and so with a sigh of despair began my course up the fearful torrent-way. To me it seemed half-a-mile at least of sliding water above me, but in truth it was little more than a furlong, as I came to know afterwards. It would have been a hard ascent, even without the slippery slime, and the force of the river over it, and I had scanty hope indeed of ever winning the summit. Nevertheless my terror left me, now I was face to face with it, and had to meet the worst; and I set myself to do my best, with a vigour and sort of hardness, which did not then surprise me, but have done so ever since.

The water was only six inches deep, or from that to nine at the utmost, and all the way up I could see my feet looking white in the gloom of the hollow, and here and there I found resting-place, to hold on by the cliff and pant awhile. And gradually as I went on, a warmth of courage breathed in me, to think that perhaps no other had dared to try that pass before me, and to wonder what mother would say to it. And then came thought of my father also, and the pain of my feet abated.

How I went carefully, step by step, keeping my arms in front of me, and never daring to straighten my knees, is more than I can tell clearly, or even like now to think of, because it makes me dream of it. Only I must acknowledge, that the greatest danger of all was just where I saw no jeopardy, but ran up a patch of black ooze-weed in a very boastful manner, being now not far from the summit.

Here I fell very piteously, and was like to have broken my kneecap, and the torrent got hold of my other leg, while I was indulging the bruised one. And then a vile knotting of cramp disabled me, and for a while I could only roar, till my mouth was full of water, and all of my body was sliding. But the fright of that brought me to again, and my elbow caught in a rock-hole; and so I managed to start again, with the help of more humility.

Now being in the most dreadful fright, because I was so near the top, and hope was beating within me, I laboured hard with both legs and arms, going like a mill, and grunting. At last the rush of forked water, where first it came over the lips of the fall, drove me into the middle, and I stuck awhile with my toe-balls on the slippery links of the pop-weed, and the world was green and gliddery, and I durst not look behind me. Then I made up my mind to die at last; for so my legs would ache no more, and my breath not pain my heart so; only it did seem such a pity, after fighting so long, to give in, and the light was coming upon me, and again I fought towards it; then suddenly I felt fresh air, and fell into it headlong.

LORNA DOONE, R.D. BLACKMORE (1869)

Blackmore, surprised at the novel's success, admitted that had he known the result would be an avalanche of visitors, which continues unabated to this day, he would have taken more care with his locations and descriptions. To the vast majority of tourists it matters very little for few of them have read the novel, and even fewer will walk up Badgworthy Water far enough to reach the supposed Doone Valley, or go in search of the water slide.

One writer does little to encourage exploration. On the contrary, Mr Page is positively disparaging in his remarks, as much on the fanciful beliefs held by others as on Blackmore's colourful descriptions of the scenery:

And now for the Doone Valley. There are those who say that 'Lorna Doone' should be studied before Exmoor is visited. I say, see Exmoor first and read its romance afterwards. Disillusion is never pleasant; and those who expect to find the Doone Valley the wild ravine painted by the glowing fancy of Blackmore, will be more than disappointed. For that this haunt of those terrible outlaws *is*

THE WATERSLIDE, BADGWORTHY

disappointing, and very distinctly so, no one who has visited it after a perusal of the Exmoor romance will deny; and I fear that the literary license indulged in by its author has not always met with that consideration which works of fiction are supposed to deserve. Having thus prepared the reader of 'Lorna Doone' for what he is *not* to expect, let us follow the pathway which skirts the Badgworthy Water, and approach the spot with philosophical resignation.

What a pity for the lovers of romance that the Doones had not the good taste to dwell in this beautiful glen! . . .

And down from his moorland home comes the shining river, at one moment sliding over a shelf of rock, at another tumbling helter-skelter over obstructing masses, again rippling in short reaches, where the trout may be seen in numbers sufficient to throw any properly-constituted angler into a fever. That Blackmore had this romantic spot in his mind when he described the Doone stronghold there can be little doubt, and but very little poetic exaggeration, added to a true picture of the valley, would represent the 'Glen Doone' of his pages.

The old woodland of gnarled oaks, known as Badgworthy Wood, is soon reached. I believe the Revd John Russell, the 'Jack Russell' of world-wide notoriety, that genial Nimrod of Exmoor, held that it was a Druid grove, and fancied that he could discover traces of an altar in its shadowy recesses. It is to be feared that fancy was stronger than fact. There is nothing in Badgworthy Wood in the least resembling an altar, beyond the excrescences of natural rock which occasionally protrude through the undergrowth. An unbelieving age that is, alas! fast forgetting the sporting parson, will have none of Druidism without evidence of the most satisfactory character, and refuses to adopt slabs of rock, however convenient, as places that have, in a former time, run with the blood of the victims of Britain's white-robed priests.

On the northern flank of this wood, a lovely little stream comes rushing down a glen, over a succession of rocky slopes; this is the Waterslide, up which John Ridd is supposed to have scrambled during that adventurous loach-fishing expedition, which ended in his

introduction to Lorna. As a matter of fact, he need not have climbed it at all, as the banks are easily accessible, and the torrent is no more a glassy rush of water than scores of others in the fair West Country. It is spanned, near its confluence with the Badgworthy Water, by a 'clam' of boughs overlaid with turf, which conducts the path onwards.

Beneath the steep hillside this path is followed for another mile, gradually ascending; the valley, meanwhile, losing in depth, though gaining in wildness. Presently we turn sharp to the right, past a little knoll, and find ourselves in a shallow combe, nearly blocked by some low eminences. Above, on the slope, stands an unpicturesque shepherd's cottage; below, beneath the hillocks, are some nearly undistinguishable ruins, consisting of lines of stone, which, for the most part, appear to mark the walls of enclosures. The most perfect building is represented but by the ruins of a tiny hut, about twelve feet square, with walls nowhere exceeding four feet in height. On the knoll commanding the entrance to the valley are more ruins, perhaps those of a lookout, with an incomplete enclosure uncommonly like a sheepfold. The Moor rises but a couple of hundred feet at most on either side the combe, and the slopes are of the easiest gradient. A small brook, concealed throughout part of its course by a beech hedge, runs down the bottom, falling into the main stream not far above the rough track climbing the hill towards Porlock, the so-called warpath of the Doones. Such is the valley visited every summer by many scores, nay, hundreds of people who, with dispelled visions of precipices, passes, and what not, depart sadder and wiser men, rather unjustly blaming the author of a picturesque romance, because the real and the ideal do not exactly coincide.

EXMOOR, J.L.W. PAGE (1890)

And Mr Page is not the only author to take a jaundiced view of the tale. The whole Doone romance is witheringly reduced by Mr Chadwyck Healey to a tale of tramps and poachers living rough, the last two meeting a pathetic end with Dickensian propensities good enough for a story in itself:

This secluded parish (Oare) on the western edge of Somerset, comprise an area of 4017 acres with a population numbering 80 souls from the last census. Its name is said to be derived from the Latin ora, or the anglo-saxon ord, or and ora, all equivalent to the English word 'bound' or limit. The country here is wild and romantic. There are two long valleys through which run the Oare and Badgworthy waters, and where to the south stretch the rolling heights of Exmoor. What houses there are, there were 15 in 1891, are scattered. There is no semblance of a village. The legendary highwayman of the West, Veggis or Faggus, is said to have had his headquarters—or rather his retreat—here. The 'Doones,' we must suppose, came hither with an equal desire to be as much out of sight of the law as possible. These people have been exalted almost to the dignity of history by the skill of the novelist. How many of the many readers of 'Lorna Doone' bring themselves seriously to doubt whether Sir Ensor Doone and his family of ruffians ever existed in fact, or something nearly approaching to fact? It is always sad to dispel pleasant illusions, but we find no trace of Doones such as these. Mr. Blackmore was, I believe, a son of a former rector of Oare, and no doubt he heard something of lawless people in the parish bearing the name that he has rendered famous. Now and then we hear of them. A venerable clergyman still living, who was at one time curate of Countisbury, and who has spent the greater part of his life in the West, believes that the real author of the Doone family was a fugitive from Sedgmoor fight, who only escaped hanging at the hands of Lord Jeffreys to carry on a series of petty depredations from a hovel on Exmoor. The old people on Exmoor used to tell Mr. Thornton that the last two of the Doone family perished about the year 1800. An old man and his little granddaughter set out to sing carols at Christmas, and gather a few pence. They were found together in the snow, quite dead, on the road between Simonsbath and Challacombe. So the story was told. In earlier days the Doones are said to have settled in two or three wretched huts in the combe which runs up at right angles to Badgeworthy Water, now the 'Doone Valley.' They stole ponies, sheep and poultry, and were generally a nuisance. In 1848 Mr. Thornton was shown by an old farmer in the parish an antiquated gun with which an ancestor, so the farmer declared with great satisfaction, had shot a Doone who was prowling about his farmyard by night. These stories seem to be the sort of foundation for the romance. They are probably true, and are much more credible than that any powerful body of outlaws had set up a stronghold on the moor. The King's Foresters of Exmoor would scarcely have tolerated so great an invasion of their privileges. The scanty ruins in the combe may be the last vestiges of the hovels of the Doones, but I have shown elsewhere that so far back as the time of Henry V. there were tenements in Badgeworthy, one of which was then 'decayed.' In Mr. Thornton's day, 1847–8, there were still living on Exmoor some old sheep-stealers, deer-killers, pony-stealers, poachers and smugglers, with whom, he says, he had the honour to be acquainted.

HISTORY OF PARTS OF WEST SOMERSET, C. CHADWYCK HEALEY (1901)

We will let Mr Bradley's schoolboy memories have the final word on dear Lorna. To him, and his mentor the rector of Wyndicombe, the work was unknown, and they were astonished that distinguished men of learning should be travelling to Exmoor in search of the Doone Valley. These early visitors were the first of a flood, and Bradley ends on a prophetic note:

At any rate, in the early spring of 1870, I think it was, nobody at Windycombe had ever heard of the Doones. For I was spending my first Easter vacation from college at the Rectory, and one morning the Rector and I had ridden to meet some fox-hounds near Brendon, either from Lynton or possibly those of Mr. Nicholas Snow at Oare, who began about this time I think to hunt the country. Anyway, we were jogging along behind the hounds, not yet in action, over the open country near Brendon, crossed by the Lynton and Exford road, when we ran into two pedestrians. They proved to be Dr. Ridding, then Head of Winchester, and one of his assistant masters, who was a relative of the Rector's. The recognition was of course hailed in these then untrodden wilds as a surprising and happy

THE FORD, MALMSMEAD

coincidence. It was, moreover, a spectacle utterly novel to us in those days.

'Where on earth are you going?' said the Rector when he had recovered from his astonishment.

'To the Doone Valley,' said Dr. Ridding. 'And no doubt you can put us on the right line.'

'To the *what*?' cried the Rector.

'The valley of the Doones,' repeated the other rather shortly, as if the suggestion of a joke in the Rector's tone was uncalled for.

'Never heard of such a place,' said the latter.

'What!' cried the famous headmaster, a little irritably. 'Why, the whole world's ringing with it. I suppose you have heard of the Doones?'

'Never in my life,' said the Rector, laughing.

'Good gracious!' exclaimed in one voice the two adventurers.

'Then I suppose you've never read *Lorna Doone!*' almost shouted the relative, pulling a book out of his haversack and tapping it.

'Never heard of it,' said the Rector, looking enquiringly at me, who, fresh from the outer world, as it were, might conceivably save our faces.

But neither my college acquaintances nor my people at home had ever mentioned this book, epoch-making as it proved, so far as Exmoor was concerned. Indeed, none of my college friends had ever so much as heard of Exmoor, as I had naturally good reason to know. It was of no use, and we had to confess that we knew nothing about *Lorna Doone* or any Blackmore, except a rather eccentric old parson at High Bray.

I suppose we ought to have felt crushed, but it would never have occurred to me at that time of life, or I fancy even to the Rector, that not to have read a popular novel was either here or there, nor, I must admit, does it greatly disturb me now.

'Perhaps you can direct us,' said Dr. Ridding, 'to the Badge*worthy* valley?'

'Oh! the Bad*gerry* valley (it was thus locally pronounced). Yes, of course.'

So the two departed from us under the Rector's directions, no doubt to comment on the belated condition of West-country life. Perhaps even recalling the classic tale of the old woman on Exmoor, or Dartmoor, or Wales, or the Cheviots, who greeted the news of the Restoration with the comment: 'Well, well, so the old King is dead at last!'

We little thought that this book was to mark the cleavage between the Old Exmoor and the New as regards the British public. And that never again would it be possible for enlightened souls in the next county, or indeed in any county, to say as they so often used to say to me: '*But where and what is Exmoor?*'

EXMOOR MEMORIES, A.G. BRADLEY (1926)

Selworthy Rectory, December 1886

Picture Credits

The credits and information on all of the illustrations used in the book are given in page ascending order.

frontispiece The steep ascent from Lynmouth is almost complete. A coach and four on the Countisbury road, from a postcard (D. Lock); **vi** Scarlet Pimpernel motor coach at Malmsmead, from a postcard (D. Lock); **2** Exford, from a postcard (D. Lock); **4** Castle Hill, the seat of Earl Fortescue. Drawn by Thomas Allom (*Devonshire Illustrated*); **7** Lynton: Valley of Rocks (*Lynton & Lynmouth*, The North Devon Athenaeum, Barnstaple); **8** Lynton and Lynmouth from the summer house on Lyn Cliff. Drawn by W. Rowe (*Scenery in the North of Devon*, The North Devon Athenaeum, Barnstaple); **11** Lynmouth: Glen Lyn (*Lynton & Lynmouth*, The North Devon Athenaeum, Barnstaple); **12** Lynmouth: Countisbury Hill (*Lynton & Lynmouth*, The North Devon Athenaeum, Barnstaple); **13** On the road (*On the Box Seat*, J.J. Hissey); **15** High Street, Dunster (D. Lock); **18** Lynton and Barnstaple Railway, from a postcard (The North Devon Athenaeum, Barnstaple); **22** Porlock, from a postcard (D. Lock); **24** Porlock Hill, gradient 1 in 4, from a postcard (D. Lock); **28** The cliff railway between Lynton and Lynmouth, from a postcard (D. Lock); **31** Watersmeet Bridge, Lynmouth (D. Lock); **33** Castle Rock, Lynton (D. Lock); **35** The fishing lodge **at** Watersmeet. Drawn by G. Rowe (*Scenery in the North of Devon*, The North Devon Athenaeum, Barnstaple); **39** Glenthorn, on the county border, home of the Halliday family. Drawn by E. Rowe (*Scenery in the North of Devon*, The North Devon Athenaeum, Barnstaple); **40** Staff photograph (D. Lock); **41** Culbone Church. Drawn by Alfred Dawson from a sketch by J.L.W. Page (*An Exploration of Exmoor*, J.L.W. Page, The North Devon Athenaeum, Barnstaple); **42** Porlock High Street, from a postcard (D. Lock); **44** Woody Bay, Lynton (D. Lock); **45** Old cottages, Alcombe, Minehead, from a postcard (D. Lock); **46** Bossington village, from a postcard (D. Lock); **49** Porlock Hill (D. Lock); **50** The Ship Inn, Porlock, from a postcard (D. Lock); **52** Rattling through Porlock village, from a postcard (D. Lock); **54** Porlock Weir. Drawn by Alfred Dawson (*An Exploration of Exmoor*, J.L.W. Page, The North Devon Athenaeum, Barnstaple); **57** Allerford (National Trust); **59** The Holnicote Estate thatcher at Luccombe, sharpening spars at Glebe Farm, 1920s, from a postcard (National Trust); **60** Cutcombe villagers, from a postcard (D. Lock); **64** Dunster (*An Exploration of Exmoor*, J.L.W. Page, The North Devon Athenaeum, Barnstaple); **66** Minehead (*An Exploration of Exmoor*, J.L.W. Page, The North Devon Athenaeum, Barnstaple); **69** Exford from the bridge. From a drawing by J.W. Norton ('Summer in Somerset', R. Jefferies); **70** Winsford, from a postcard (D. Lock); **71** Barlinch Priory, from a lantern slide (D. Bromwich, The Somerset Archaeological and Natural History Society); **72** An early view of Simonsbath, from a postcard (T. Bartlett); **75** Bury Bridge, from a postcard (D. Bromwich, The Taunton Local History Library, property of Mrs L.M. Lock); **78** Camp at Exebridge, 16 September 1929 (D. Lock); **81** The Vicarage, Simonsbath (T. Bartlett)' **82** Coronation of King George V celebrations, 1911, Dunkery Beacon (National Trust); **84** Exmoor from the Quantocks. Drawn by Alfred Dawson (*An Exploration of Exmoor*, J.L.W. Page); **87** Preparing for a ride on the incline of the Brendon railway (K. Astell); **89** Roadwater, 1907 (D. Bromwich, The Taunton Local History Library, property of Dr A.W.G, Court); **91** Bampfylde Copper Mine,

Picture Credits

North Molton (The North Devon Athenaeum, Barnstaple); **92** North Molton (R.L. Knight collection); **93** Ruins of mine buildings, Combe Martin (R.L. Knight collection); **95** Combe Martin. Drawn by J.M.W. Turner R.A. (The North Devon Athenaeum, Barnstaple); **97** Hunter's Inn, from a postcard (D. Lock); **101** The stag the harbourer wants to find (*Exmoor*, C. Aldin); **103** Cloutsham Farm, from a postcard (D. Lock); **105** Lord Poltimore at Twitchen with Mr Thorne and hounds (private collection); **106** Puppy judging at North Molton (private collection); **109** Hounds crossing North Molton Bridge (private collection); **112** Old Bridge, near Lynmouth, from a postcard (D. Lock); **115** Exford, from the recreation field (K. Astell); **116** Hounds meet at Dunster (K. Astell); **119** Ploughing near Watchet, from a postcard (D. Lock); **122** Threshing at Withycombe (D. Lock); **124** Winsford, from a postcard (D. Lock); **125** Hayricks at harvest time (National Trust); **127** Badgworthy Water and Doone Valley (*Lynton & Lynmouth*, The North Devon Athenaeum, Barnstaple); **131** The waterslide, Badgworthy. Drawn by Alfred Dawson (*An Exploration of Exmoor*, J.L.W. Page, The North Devon Athenaeum, Barnstaple); **134** The Ford, Malmsmead, from a postcard (D. Lock); **146** Selworthy Rectory, December 1886 (D. Lock).

Bibliography

Afghan of Porlock, 'The Charcoal Burners of Culbone', *Exmoor Review*. 1962

C. Aldin, *Exmoor: the Riding Playground of England*. London, H.F. & G. Witherby, 1935.

Anon., *Echoes of Exmoor*. London, Simpkin, Marshall, Hamilton and Kent, 1925.

S. Baring-Gould, *A Book of the West*. London, Methuen, 1899.

Bell's Pocket Guide to Devon. London, 1929.

J. Billingsley, *General View of Agriculture of the County of Somerset, with Observation on the Means of its Improvements*. Bath, Cruttwel, 1795.

R.D. Blackmore, *Lorna Doone*. London, Sampson Low, 1869.

A.G. Bradley, *Exmoor Memories*. London, Methuen, 1926.

British Medical Association, *Book of the South West*. Wm Pollard, 1907.

E. Burritt, *A Walk from London to Land's End and Back*. London, Sampson Low, 1834.

C. Chadwyck Healey, *History of Parts of West Somerset*. London, Henry Southern, 1901.

J. Collinson, *History and Antiquities of the County of Somerset*. Bath, Cruttwell, 1791.

P. Evered, *Staghunting with the Devon and Somerset*. Exeter and London, Chatto & Windus, 1902.

T. Gerard, *Particular Description of the County of Somersett*. Somerset Record Society, 1900.

W. Gilpin, *Observations on the Western Parts of England*. London, Cadell & Davis, 1798.

W. Gresswell, *Forests and Deer Parks of the County of Somerset*. Taunton, Barnicott & Pearce, 1905.

C.G. Harper, *The North Devon Coast*. London, Chapman & Hall, 1908.

Heath, 'The Romance of Peasant Life', *The Morning Advertiser*. July 1873.

J.J. Hissey, *On the Box Seat*. London, Richard Bentley, 1886.

R. Jefferies, *Red Deer*. London, Longman, 1884.

——, 'Summer in Somerset', *English Illustrated Magazine*. 1887.

M.H. Jones, *Extracts from a Brendon Hill Diary*. 1865.

J. Leland, *John Leland's Itinerary*. 1543.

B. Little, *The Monmouth Episode*. London, Werner Laurie, 1956.

G. Lye, *Glenthorne Diary*. 1904.

D. Lyson, *Topographical and Historical Account of Devonshire*. 1822.

D. Lysons, *Magna Britannica*. London, Thomas Cadell, 1822.

S.P.B. Mais, *Glorious Devon*. London, Great Western Railways, 1928.

H.J. Marshall, *Rural Economy of the West of England*. London, Eyre & Spottiswoode, 1948.

W. Marshall, *Rural Economy of the West of England*. London, G. Nicol, 1796.

W.G. Maton, *Observations of the Western Counties*. Salisbury, Easton, 1794.

Murrays's Handbook. 1865.

J.L.W. Page, *The Coasts of Devon*. 1895.

——, *Exmoor*. 1890.

——, *Exploration of the Coast of North Devon*. 1893.

J.H.B. Peel, *Country Talk Again*. London, Robert Hale, 1970.

R. Polwhele, *History of Devonshire*. 1806 (reprinted Dorking, Kohler, 1977).

Bibliography

J. Presland, *Lynton and Lynmouth*. London, Chatto & Windus, 1918.

W. Sherracombe, *Exmoor*. London, Heath Cranton, 1920.

J.M. Slader, *Days of Renown*. Bracknell, West Country Publications, 1965.

F.J. Snell, *Book of Exmoor*. London, Methuen, 1903.

Southey.

W.H. Thompson, *Devon Coast, Moors and Rivers* (foreword by Hon. John Fortescue). University of London, 1932.

W.H. Thornton, *Reminiscences and Reflections of an Old West Country Clergyman*. Torquay, Andrew & Iredale, 1899.

W.J. Turner, *Exmoor Village*. London, George Harrop, 1947.

Victoria History of Somerset. London, James Street, 1911.

C.F. Wade, *Exmoor Streams and Angling Notes*. London, Chatto & Windus, 1903.

Ward Lock, *Red Guide*. London, Ward Lock 1911.

R. Warner, *Walks through Wales and the Western Counties*. Bath, Crutwell, 1799.

J. Wesley, Diaries. 1744–77.

W. Wilkinson, *The Peep Show*. 1927.

T.H. Williams and T. Johns, *Picturesque Excursions in Devonshire and Cornwall*. London, John Murray, 1804.

H. Williamson, 'Country of the Rain', *Lone Swallows*. London, G. Putnam, 1930.

Index

Index

Mole, River, 69

Molland, 7, 13, 69, 75, 93

Molton, North, 5, 7, 69, 90, 93

Molton, South, 3, 75, 90, 91, 99, 111

Morning Advertiser, 56

Murray's Handbook, 32, 82, 83, 86

Newnes, G., 12

Oare, 25, 39, 133

Old Barrow, 36, 37

Page, J.L.W., 12, 28, 52, 66, 85, 94, 95, 97, 125, 131, 132

Parracombe, 43, 100, 114, 118

Peel, J.H.B., 62, 117, 120, 121

Pinkery Pond, 68

Poltimore, 93

Polwhele, Revd R., 76

Porlock, 1, 21, 24, 27, 41, 42, 45, 46, 48, 49, 50, 52, 53, 55, 56, 65, 66, 77, 80, 86, 108, 113, 125

Presland, J., 28, 34, 48, 63

Prince of Wales, 104, 106, 108, 110

Punch and Judy, 20, 25

Raleighs Cross, 88

Red Guide, 57, 95

Russell, Jack, 104, 106, 110, 132

Selworthy, 57, 65

Shelley, P.B., 28, 29

Sherracombe, W., 43, 116

Simonsbath, 2, 26, 69, 80, 82, 85, 86, 91, 99, 100

Slader, J.M., 90, 91, 93

Snell, F.J., 7, 9, 104

Southey, 3, 28, 29, 48

Stoke Pero, 59, 66

Tarr Steps, 68, 73, 110

Thornton, Revd W, 7, 9, 26, 37, 47, 133

Timberscombe, 13

Trentishoe, 97, 115

Turner, W.J. 63

Valley of Rocks, 5, 16, 17, 114

Wade, C., 111, 113, 114

Warner, Revd. R., 7, 52

Watchet, 86

Watersmeet, 30, 34, 112

Wesley, John, 5, 7

West Somerset Polo Club, 55, 113

Wilkinson, W., 20, 25

Williamson, H., 57, 68, 117

Windycombe, 19, 20

Winsford, 9, 66, 69, 70

Withypool, 77

Woody Bay, 43

Wordsorth, W., 3, 28, 29

Wotton Courtney, 59

Yarner, 42